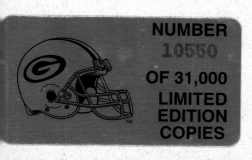

Titletown
AGAIN

The Super Bowl Season of the 1996 Green Bay Packers

By Chuck Carlson
Introduction by Bob Harlan
Foreword by Mike Holmgren
Photography by Vernon and Jim Biever

PACKERS

Dedication

To the loyal, patient and slightly obsessed fans of the Green Bay Packers. The team was right, part of that Vince Lombardi Trophy belongs to you, too.

Bob Snodgrass
Publisher

Vernon Biever and Jim Biever
Photo Editors

Steve Cameron
Managing Editor

Brad Breon
Publishing Consultant

Darcie Kidson
Publicity

Randy Breeden
Art Direction/Design

Dust jacket and soft cover design by Jerry Hirt
Cover photo by Chris Dennis
Production Assistance: Michelle Washington, Sharon Snodgrass, Chip Power, David Power
Contributing Photographers: Scott Cunningham, Chris Dennis, Russ Reaver, Allen Fredrickson, Steve Gibson
Select photos courtesy of the Green Bay Packers.

Published by Addax Publishing Group, Lenexa, Kansas
Printed and bound in Canada

Distributed to the trade by Andrews & McMeel, 4520 Main Street, Kansas City, Missouri 64111

Library of Congress Catalog Card Number: 97-70764
ISBN: 0-886110-23-9 (Collectors Edition, Leather)
ISBN: 0-886110-21-2 (Limited Edition, Hardback)
ISBN: 0-886110-22-0 (General Edition, Paperback)

Author's Acknowledgments

The mobilization it took to get this project off the ground, rolling and completed in such a short period of time would have made the Normandy Invasion look like a trip to the grocery store. And for that, I have to thank a lot of people.

It starts, of course, with the Green Bay Packers organization and its president, Bob Harlan, who showed the faith to let me chronicle the Packers' remarkable season.

Special thanks go out to coach Mike Holmgren, his staff and coaches, general manager Ron Wolf and the players, without whom, naturally, there would be no need for such a book.

An especially deep appreciation goes out to Lee Remmel, the Packers estimable public relations director, who offered help, advice, suggestions and direction at the critical junctures and helped make this book something special.

Thanks also to Lee's dedicated PR staff of Jeff Blumb, Lee's able second in command, Mark Schiefelbein, Aaron Popkey, Paula Martin and Linda McCrossin. As well, thanks to Jeff Cieply, the Packers marketing director.

Then there are the folks from Addax Publishing, most especially publisher Bob Snodgrass and his computer-whiz of a wife, Sharon, who taught me the difference between WordPerfect 5.1 and 6.0. And for that, I'm grateful. I think.

Also many thanks to Brad Breon, Darcie Kidson and Michelle Washington from Addax.

I also owe a debt to my employers at The *Post-Crescent* in Appleton, Wisconsin. Thanks to associate publisher Kevin Doyle, managing editor Bill Knutson, football writer Tom Mulhern and my sports editor, Larry Gallup, who gave me the time to put this project together the right way.

To photographers Vernon and Jim Biever, Chris Dennis, Russ Reaver and Chip Power, thanks as well. And don't worry Chris, those photos you took in the French Quarter won't see the light of day.

Then there's my editor Steve Cameron, my mentor and scourge, who still doesn't understand my subtle turn of phrases but did a splendid job in a short time under trying circumstances anyway. I also have to thank Steve for moving to Provo, Utah and giving me the chance to write this book. I owe him a lot. Unfortunately, he knows it, too.

Finally, a deep bow to my long-suffering wife Theresa, who waded through a long Packers season and an even longer Super Bowl week and still maintained something resembling good humor. I owe her too. And she also knows it.

Chuck Carlson

Contents

Introduction
By Robert E. Harlan
February 6, 1997

N 1960, WHEN I HAD JUST GRADUATED FROM MARQUETTE UNIVERSITY AND WAS WORKING as sports information director at Marquette, just getting started in public relations, I attended a Packer game at Milwaukee County Stadium. I made a comment to my wife then that I hoped I could grow in the public relations field and become competent enough that some day I might become the public relations director for the Green Bay Packers....When the opportunity came along, eleven years later, to join this fine organization, I jumped at it.

And now, a quarter century later, I am most happy that I did. If I hadn't, I would have deprived myself of a rewarding career and a remarkable experience....highlighted by sharing in a hallmark 1996 season and the joy and exultation of the Packers' historic victory over the New England Patriots in Super Bowl XXXI.

Today, as president of the Green Bay Packers, a position I never dreamed of having when I joined the organization, it is virtually impossible to put the depth of those emotions into words. It had been almost three decades since the Packers had won a Super Bowl and I'm sure there were those who thought it might never happen again. When it did, it was almost too good to be true.

Indeed, what the 1996 Packers achieved under the leadership of Ron Wolf and the direction of Head Coach Mike Holmgren – in these days of free agency and the salary cap – is truly remarkable, winning more games in a single season (16) than any other team in the organization's 78–year history and climaxing a magical year with a decisive triumph in the Super Bowl.

Certainly, I am happy for myself, because I am – and always will be – a Packer fan. But my greatest satisfaction has come in the sheer delight the Super Bowl victory and world championship have brought to our fans, the most loyal I have ever known.

I also am pleased that the rewarding story of the '96 season is being told...in depth...in the colorful pages of *Titletown AGAIN*...the story of a team with a mission and an unswerving focus...a team that is certain to take its rightful place in the organization's rich history, alongside those champions of the late '30s and the highly successful '60s.

It is a book, I am convinced, that every Packer loyalist will want to have – a book that will enable each of them to re–live the '96 season...big play by big play and victory by victory...for the rest of their lives.

Robert E. Harlan

Bob Harlan
President and CEO
Green Bay Packers

Foreword
Titletown Again
Mike Holmgren

BEFORE WE OPENED TRAINING CAMP LAST JULY, I REMEMBER SAYING, "THE NEXT LOGICAL step for us...on paper...is the Super Bowl because we made it to the NFC Championship Game last year."

But saying that, I was well aware as I spoke, does not make it a reality. Having been through the demanding process as an assistant coach, I knew that bringing such a "step" to fruition requires a collective and season–long commitment from players, coaches, front office and support staff, as well as consistent and high level performance on the field. And, certainly, good physical fortune.

Then, if you have all of those elements going for you, it gives you a chance to get to the Super Bowl. Having been involved in that experience twice while on the San Francisco coaching staff, I knew that there are so many factors in getting to the Super Bowl other than the fact that you have to be a good team...Basically, you have to be lucky AND good.

But, bottom line, I believe the team concept – an unselfish, "one–for–all and all–for–one" approach from the players – invariably is the key to any successful season, and any successful team. In this league, very rarely can you just win on talent...straight, out–and–out talent. And I think you need chemistry or feeling...or whatever it might be called...You need that team feeling.

And, in 1996, we had that, to as great an extent as I have ever seen. You need guys rooting for each other on the sideline and, throughout the season, I heard that. There was an unselfish feeling – no one was overly concerned about who got the credit. And it was also true of my coaching staff.

The end result was a season that, as a coach, you dream about. So I, for one, am pleased that the story of the '96 Packers and their Super Bowl season is being told in the pages and pictures of *Titletown AGAIN* – a permanent record of a memorable year for all of us to share and enjoy.

From a personal perspective, I would like to dedicate this book to "The Team" – and, in equal tribute, to the world's greatest fans. It was a season that I hope every Packer fan will long remember...It also is one that I will never forget.

Mike Holmgren
Head Coach
Green Bay Packers

Chapter 1

The Long Road to New Orleans

T

O UNDERSTAND HOW THE GREEN BAY PACKERS WON SUPER BOWL XXXI on January 26, 1997 over the New England Patriots at the Louisiana Superdome, it's important – no, make that crucial – to go back 378 days to January 14, 1996.

Remember?

The Packers, to a man, certainly do.

Green Bay Packers vs. Dallas Cowboys.

Texas Stadium. NFC championship. For the Packers, it was a day that will live in infamy.

They remember the ache, the emptiness, the futility of walking off the Texas Stadium field at the conclusion of the NFC Championship Game having lost, again, to the Cowboys, 38-27.

For the Packers, losing to the Cowboys was nothing new, since they'd done it five times in the previous two seasons before that game. But those times were different because, deep down, despite all the brave talk, the Packers knew they were inferior to the Cowboys. Dallas was bigger, stronger, faster, more experienced and – well, better – than Green Bay.

The Packers always had that to comfort them during those long, cold off-seasons.

But on that January evening in 1996, the Packers figured they'd turned the tide.

Coach Mike Holmgren and general manager Ron Wolf finally had put together a team that could compete with anyone, including the Cowboys.

They had an offense triggered by Brett Favre, the league's most valuable player. They had dangerous receivers in wideout Robert Brooks and tight ends Mark Chmura and Keith Jackson, and they had a competent defense.

This, the Packers felt, was the year.

But for three quarters, that's exactly how the Packers played, matching the Cowboys score for score, play for play. They had even faced crushing adversity during the game when wide receivers coach Gil Haskell was taken off the field in an ambulance after suffering a serious head injury. Haskell's head hit the stadium floor after he was knocked down during a play that carried out of bounds.

But the Packers put it all behind them and, heading into the fourth quarter, Green Bay led 27-24 – the first time these particular Packers ever had led Dallas in the final period.

And it turned out to be a cruel hoax.

In the final 10 minutes, the Packers saw their dream of a Super Bowl dissolve under the weight of two Cowboys touchdowns. They had cracked under pressure at the

Brett Favre and coach Mike Holmgren address the media in July.

▶ **Brett Favre, reported to training camp in the best shape in his life, a fact noted by coach Mike Holmgren.**

John Michels, a 285-pound left tackle from the University of Southern California, was the Packers' No. 1 draft pick in April. The plan was to have Michels learn at the knee of veteran Ken Ruettgers and then take over in 1997. But Ruettgers was slow to recover from off–season knee surgery and Michels was thrown into the fire quickly. He made his initial appearance in the preseason opener Aug. 2., ironically, against the New England Patriots. "I stayed vertical," Favre said afterward. "So I guess he did a pretty good job."

Another new face belonged to safety Eugene Robinson, who was traded to the Packers in June for backup defensive end Matt LaBounty. Though a 12–year veteran and two years removed from a serious Achilles tendon injury, Green Bay felt so good about Robinson that they traded their safety of the last two seasons, the popular George Teague, to Atlanta.

worst time. They had shown, briefly at least, that they were contenders. But in the end, they still lacked a certain something.

"We fell apart," Green Bay defensive end Sean Jones said.

Then, when it was over, they had to watch as the Cowboys crowed to the world about how dominant they were.

That really hurt.

Yet it was a hurt the Packers swore to themselves they'd never forget and, more important, that they would use as a learning tool.

"Remember how this feels," Holmgren told his players. "Don't ever forget it."

Even on the long, long plane ride back, Holmgren walked up and down the aisle telling his players to keep their heads up and never forget.

"He told us, 'We didn't get it done this time, but we're going to get there,' " safety LeRoy Butler recalled. "We all vowed to come back in the best shape of our lives and do whatever it took to get back. That's all we thought about."

Of course, it's one thing to vow a comeback after falling short. Every team in every sport does that. What would they have to play for if they didn't?

The Packers, though, turned that hurt, that longing in Dallas into something tangible.

By the time training camp opened in July of 1996, they spoke unabashedly about where they planned to go.

"It's the Super Bowl or bust," quarterback Brett Favre said.

Still, there were questions. So many questions.

Leading the list, of course, was Favre himself. He had stunned the Packers and football in general when he announced in May that he was going into a drug rehabilitation clinic because of an addiction to a painkiller.

Second–year defensive tackle Darius Holland showed flashes in his rookie year that he could be a dependable player for the Packers. But he faded toward the end of the season and played little. Green Bay knew he'd have to come through in 1996 if the defense was going to be successful.

An intriguing player was wide receiver Derrick Mayes, Green Bay's No. 2 draft pick out of Notre Dame. He had a brilliant training camp, making acrobatic catches and doing a solid job returning punts. But he struggled to learn the offense, as most rookies do.

He talked about suffering a seizure in a Green Bay hospital, a terrifying moment that his eight-year-old daughter Brittany watched in horror and then asked if daddy was going to die.

It was incredible. Unthinkable. And as a chastened Favre spoke, Packer fans saw the season going down the drain four months before it even started.

Could Favre rebound and produce the kind of numbers he had the year before, when he earned the MVP award and nearly single-handedly carried the team? Could he curb his

kamikaze ways so he wouldn't get beat up so much? Would teams intentionally try to hurt him now that he was vulnerable?

Anything was possible and until he proved otherwise, Favre was the biggest question mark on this team.

There were others.

The defense, which had shown signs of improvement in '95 but caved in under Dallas' title-game assault, needed to be even better if the Packers planned to go anywhere in the playoffs.

Defensive end Reggie White had looked mortal the season before after suffering a torn hamstring. His numbers also dipped and there was some question if he was still the player he'd been. What about the secondary, which had been shredded the year before? Could Craig Newsome and Doug Evans do the job on the corners? Could Butler at safety recapture his Pro Bowl status of two years earlier? And what about the new guy, Eugene Robinson, who was acquired in a trade? Did Robinson, at age 33, still have anything left?

Could Gilbert Brown finally stay healthy at nose tackle and have the kind of season everyone thought he was capable of having? Was free agent tackle Santana Dotson just looking for the right scheme to play or was he already on the downside of his career as his stats at Tampa Bay seemed to show?

And then what about the linebacker corps? Fred Strickland was gone from the middle and somebody had to step in. But who? Was free agent Ron Cox, late of the Chicago Bears, the answer? What about George Koonce? How did the gifted Brian Williams fit in the picture?

On offense, the Packers also needed answers to their line problems.

Would veteran Ken Ruettgers recover from off-season knee surgery in time to return to his familiar left tackle spot? Or would No. 1 draft pick John Michels be thrown to the wolves? Packers fans (and coaches, for that matter) shuddered at the possibility of a rookie protecting Favre's blind side on pass plays.

Could Keith Jackson and Mark Chmura co-exist at tight end? Could second-year wide receiver Antonio Freeman step in at split end to complement flanker Robert Brooks? Was the running game in decent hands with Edgar

Bennett, the game, but limited halfback?

So many questions.

And that didn't even take into account the fact that the Packers were going to play the toughest schedule in the NFL, a brutal march featuring five teams that had made the playoffs the year before – Philadelphia, San Diego, San Francisco, Kansas City and Dallas – and two mind-numbing, three-game road trips.

"It's obvious the NFL doesn't want us to win the Super Bowl with a schedule like that," Favre said more than once.

But through all of that, the expectations were soaring because if most of those questions were resolved with satisfactory answers, the Packers could indeed go all the way.

And they knew it.

They were so sure, in fact, that talk of the Super Bowl crept into players' vocabularies from the start of spring mini-camps until the regular season opener, when an exasperated Holmgren put a halt to it.

"No more Super Bowl talk," he told his team early in the season.

Just because they weren't talking about it, though, didn't mean they weren't thinking about it.

"That's our motivation," Evans said. "We know how good we can be."

But the pieces would have to fall together and the chemistry would have to be something approaching perfection. Everyone had to know his role and where he fit into the grand scheme on this team.

"It all boils down to how they feel they're contributing," Holmgren said. "These are guys who are not particularly selfish and they don't want the ball every time. But they do want to know that they're contributing and that they're part of the success."

And Holmgren, with the help of his team leaders, had to find that perfect balance.

There were stars on this team and everyone knew who they were. Favre, Brooks, White, Butler. They could be counted on to do their jobs.

The key to the season, though, certainly would turn on how the role players did their jobs. Where would fullbacks Dorsey Levens and William Henderson fit in? Could free agent Don Beebe be a No. 3 receiver? Or Terry

Mickens? Would Gabe Wilkins step up when White had to come out for a breather? Could the sometimes-petulant Wayne Simmons continue the incredible linebacking play he'd shown the previous postseason?

And what about Sean Jones, the one-time star defensive end with Houston and Los Angeles Raiders? Could he adapt to his new role as a run-stopper? Would he pout at having to take a $1,000,000 pay cut to help with the salary cap?

Holmgren thought he knew the answers to all of this. At least he hoped he did.

Grizzled veteran safety Mike Prior was the epitome of this Packers team. Relegated to a backup role two years earlier, he accepted his position, even taking a paycut to stay in Green Bay, and proceeded to produce several huge plays in 1996.

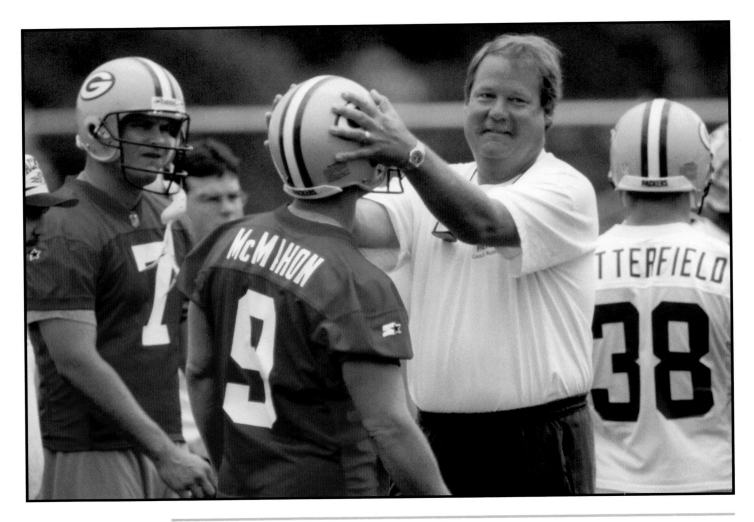

▲ Though he
played sparingly,
quarterback Jim
McMahon, a
veteran of 15
seasons and seven
teams, put coach
Mike Holmgren's
mind at ease by
giving him a
veteran backup for
Brett Favre.

The early glimpses were promising, too, as Green Bay roared to three impressive preseason wins over New England, Pittsburgh and Baltimore. But a rout at the hands of Indianapolis in the exhibition finale left an uncertainty in Holmgren.

Favre had not played particularly well in the preseason. Then again, he was never asked to do much. The No. 1 defense had been OK, but not dominating. The running game was still in flux and the receiving unit remained up in the air.

Then came the season-opening bombing of the Tampa Bay Buccaneers and all the nagging questions seemed to melt away in the stifling humidity of Florida.

Five months later, the journey ended in New Orleans as the Green Bay Packers were crowned the NFL's best team.

How did they do it?

Tough question.

It started with the realization that if they were to be successful, every player had to play to his maximum level every week. And in a 16-week schedule, that's not an easy task.

Yes, the Packers got lucky, too, suffering no major injuries on defense and only one season-ending injury on offense – to Brooks.

But perhaps more than anything, this was a team that would not be denied. The focus that many teams seem to lose at some point in the season didn't desert the Packers.

Resolute, driven, relentless.

The Packers went through this season as though they were on a mission. And in truth, they were.

"Our goal all year was to get to the Super Bowl and win it," Freeman said. "That's all that was ever on our minds. Anything less and the season would have been a failure."

The season was not a failure.

Chapter 1

▶ **Though he didn't know it during preseason, coach Mike Holmgren (left) would find a lot to be happy with in special teams coach Nolan Cromwell.**

Chapter 2
Favre And Away
September 1: Packers 34, Buccaneers 3

THE QUESTIONS SWIRLED AROUND BRETT FAVRE LIKE SNOW FLURRIES IN A Green Bay December.

Could he do it? Would he do it? What did he have left? What would happen the first time the Green Bay Packers' franchise player took a big-time hit in a game situation?

So many questions. So few answers. And there was nothing the Packers or their fans could do but wait and see what happened.

Wait and worry, and maybe say a small prayer.

After all, there may be no team in the NFL that ties its fortunes so completely to one player the way the Packers have to Favre over the past few seasons.

But all that was thrown into turmoil when Favre made the stunning announcement that he would enter a drug rehabilitation clinic to help kick an addiction to a prescription painkiller.

Suddenly, the league's reigning MVP looked vulnerable and beatable and human. And so did the Packers, who had come into the 1996 season as one of the favorites to reach the Super Bowl.

Favre spent 46 days in the Menninger Clinic in Topeka, Kansas, cleaning himself up and beating back his demons. And when he returned shortly before training camp, he trumpeted the news that he was better than ever. In better shape. In a better frame of mind. A better player.

Packers fans crossed their fingers and waited for evidence.

Yet by the time the season got started for real Sept. 1 in Tampa, they were still waiting.

In limited duty during four preseason games, Favre had not looked particularly sharp. He seemed skittery and nervous in the pocket, he overthrew open receivers and he didn't have the snap, the spark or the swagger he'd displayed the season before.

So as the season began in sultry Tampa, the questions that had hung over Favre and the Packers for weeks were still there.

But when Favre took the field for pregame warmups, he was like a little kid again. He looked up to the sky during a thundershower and smiled, opening his mouth to let the rain in and, perhaps, to prove that football was still a game.

All the questions, concerns and consternation melted away over the course of a three-hour demolition of the Buccaneers.

Favre completed 20 of 27 passes for 247 yards and four touchdowns – three in the first half alone to Keith Jackson. Favre didn't throw an interception as he made what was easily his most impressive season debut as a Packer.

It all started in the first quarter.

Already leading 3-0, the Packers forced a turnover on the Tampa Bay 27. Two plays later, Favre hit a sliding Jackson in the back of the end zone for the 1-yard touchdown. It was

---

Questions about Packers quarterback Brett Favre abounded as he prepared for the 1996 season. His 46-day stay in a drug rehabilitation clinic in the spring had caused many to wonder if he could regain his MVP form of the previous season. Favre's response? "Bet against me," he said.

▶ Flanker Robert Brooks (left) and split end Antonio Freeman made a lethal combination at wide receiver for the Packers until Brooks was lost for the season with a knee injury at midseason against the 49ers. Still, in the opener against Tampa Bay, the two combined to catch nine passes for 107 yards.

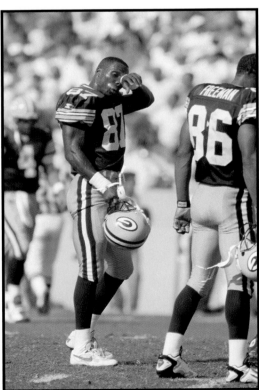

Tampa, Fla. in September is not exactly the frozen tundra. And there were many who thought the heat and stifling humidity of Florida would force the Packers to wilt in the season-opener. For wide receiver Robert Brooks, it was indeed warm work but as defensive end Sean Jones proves, they were cool all day in posting the 34-3 win.

the first of what would be Favre's club-record 39 touchdown passes that season.

The second touchdown came with 1:40 left in the second quarter when Favre again found Jackson, this time for a 4-yard score.

The Packers promptly got the ball back once more on their own 49 before the end of the half and Favre made the Buccaneers pay, as he slid away from pressure and found Jackson embarrassingly wide open in the middle of the field. Jackson stepped out of an attempted Charles Dimry tackle and scored on the 51-yard pass play that put the final stake through the Bucs' hearts.

Favre added a 1-yard touchdown toss to fullback Dorsey Levens in the fourth quarter to dress up his already glittering statistics.

The Packers' Super Bowl caravan had begun to the tune of 34-3 over Tampa Bay.

Afterward, Favre and the rest of the Packers basked in the notion that they had proved all those critics wrong.

With the guidance of veteran secondary coach Bob Valesente, second-year cornerback Craig Newsome improved by leaps and bounds in 1996.

Brett Favre wasted no time in showing he was as good as ever, throwing for 247 yards and four touchdowns against the hapless Buccaneers.

"There were questions about me?" Favre said facetiously and with more than a little steel in his voice. "I think that question's answered. I told you guys (the media) a long time ago to bet against me. I don't know where your money is, but..."

He never finished the sentence. He didn't have to.

The sentiment was echoed by his teammates.

"We told you guys he was going to be the same old Brett," wide receiver Robert Brooks said.

"Same old Brett," repeated tight end Mark Chmura, one of Favre's best friends.

"I would have been more surprised if he didn't play well," coach Mike Holmgren said.

This was clearly sweet vindication for Favre, who never felt he got the credit he deserved for the incredible season he'd had the year before, when he was the league's most valuable player.

He may have had a chip on his shoulder, but he felt if anybody deserved one, it was him.

"We answered a lot of questions," Jackson said. "This was a good first step to the Super Bowl."

But it was just one step in a long, long journey.

Monday Night Madness
September 9: Packers 39, Eagles 13

THE NEXT STEP CAME IN THE SURREAL CIRCUS ATMOSPHERE THAT WAS Lambeau Field.

It wasn't the usual hysteria that normally accompanies a Packers home game. This one was special. This one was different. For the first time in 10 years, Lambeau was hosting a Monday night game and the electricity generated could have lit every lightbulb from Green Bay to Milwaukee for years.

It was more than a football game. At least it was for the Packers and their fans. It was almost a validation of what they'd done and how far they'd come over the past four years.

Team president Bob Harlan said it best when in the week before the game, he admitted that he was getting tired of playing at noon every Sunday. The good teams, the really good ones, got on the Monday night show.

After seven years away from the bright lights, the Packers had flashed onto the ABC prime-time stage in 1993, for a road game with the Kansas City Chiefs that they lost, 23-16.

Still, they played well enough and showed the league that they deserved a return invitation the next year. And in hurricane-like conditions at Soldier Field, the Packers routed their ancient rivals, the Chicago Bears, 33-6.

In '95, the Pack returned to Chicago for a Monday night encore.

In that one, Green Bay bolted to a 27-7 third quarter lead, then watched as the Bears attempted a furious comeback that eventually fell short, 27-24.

Clearly, the Packers had proven they were a marquee talent that could handle the unique pressure that is Monday Night Football.

And it truly was special that, finally, the road show was at least coming back to Lambeau Field.

"This means everything to us," coach Mike Holmgren said. "I think it shows just how far this team has come."

It also meant that the rest of the league, and the rest of the country, would be watching, too.

The Packers knew only too well that they were still something of a regional obsession. They had loyal, crazy fans, fans who would die for their Packers. But to most of the rest of the football world, the Green Bay Packers remained a quaint novelty. This was a nice little team that had a pretty good quarterback, a solid coach and the kind of foundation you can build winners on.

The only real national exposure they'd received was in the playoffs, where they usually played Dallas and where they always lost.

But this would be different.

The Philadelphia Eagles, a playoff team from 1995 and a crew that harbored some Super Bowl aspirations of their own, were the visitors.

There were more than a few sub-plots in that as well.

The Eagles' head coach was the sometimes volcanic Ray Rhodes. Rhodes was in his second season as the Eagles' head guy and he had worked wonders. In his first season, he'd led a ragtag unit to a 10-6 record and earned NFL coach of the year honors.

Defensive end Reggie White (right) and tackle Santana Dotson celebrate sacking Eagles' quarterback Rodney Peete for a safety. Dotson, signed as a free agent from Tampa Bay, gave the Packers the interior pass rush they had lacked in years past and offered a complement to ends White and Sean Jones.

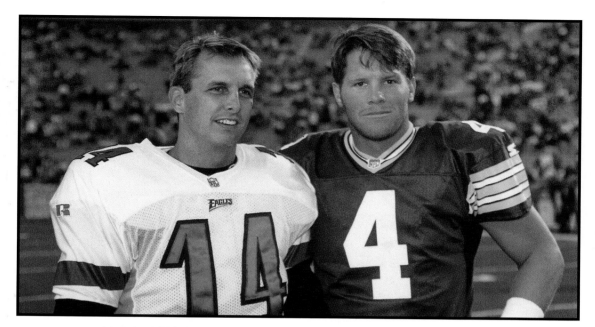

Brett Favre and former teammate Ty Detmer get together before the game. Detmer saw the writing on the wall and, after four seasons of backing up Favre, signed as a free agent with the Eagles prior to the 1996 season. Two games later, Detmer took over the starting role and led Philadelphia to the playoffs.

He topped it by crushing Detroit in the play-offs before finally falling to Dallas.

Yet the truly intriguing element was that Holmgren and Rhodes had gone way back as assistant coaches with the San Francisco 49ers.

The two men had grown close over the years, as Holmgren had first worked with the Niners quarterbacks and then became offensive coordinator while Rhodes tutored San Francisco's running backs and then wide receivers.

When Holmgren was hired by the Packers as head coach, one of his first moves was to bring Rhodes with him as defensive coordinator.

After two seasons, Rhodes went back to the 49ers as defensive coordinator and then a year later, he took the top job with the Eagles.

Stories flew every which way about why Rhodes left Green Bay so abruptly. Some thought he'd had a philosophical falling out with Holmgren. Others believed his family couldn't adjust to the mostly white Green Bay social scene. Still others felt the 49ers had lured him away in revenge for the Packers taking Holmgren as their head coach.

There were little mini-dramas to this matchup, including former Packer quarterback Ty Detmer now playing with the Eagles after signing as a free agent the previous spring; Green Bay defensive end Reggie White, a one-time Eagle who still had deep feeling for the

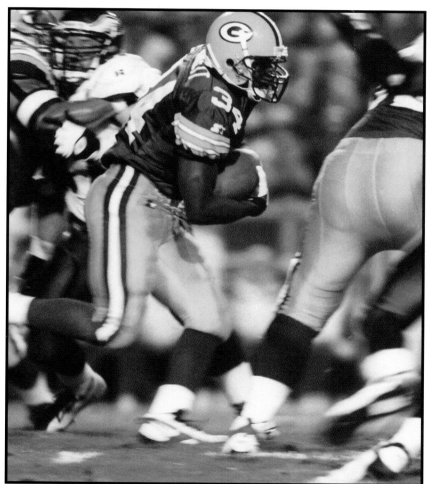

▲ Halfback Edgar Bennett slashes through the Philadelphia line for a sizeable gain. It proved to be one of his best games of the season as he rushed for 93 yards and caught a season-high five passes for 49 more yards and a touchdown.

▲ The Packers wait in their tunnel to be introduced before the Monday night game. It was the first Monday nighter at Lambeau Field in 10 years and the sellout crowd was in all its raucous glory.

▶ Craig Hentrich unloads a punt against the Eagles. Another unsung player, Hentrich averaged 42.4 yards per kick, held for placekicker Chris Jacke and took over kickoff duties.

organization; and others.

Ultimately, however, none of that mattered.

The Packers knew they needed this game to establish themselves as a serious force and that's exactly the way they approached it.

As a result, it was no contest.

Carried by waves of emotion and noise that rocked the old stadium, the Packers showed a national TV audience that they had to be taken seriously after all, pounding the Eagles, 39-13, improving to 2-0 for the first time since 1982.

"I asked for a little extra from our fans and they certainly did that," Holmgren said. "I wanted it to be a celebration and have a great evening here in Green Bay, our first Monday night game in a while. It was all of those things. And then we won the game to boot. It was a great evening for us."

Favre, who completed 17 of 31 passes for 261 yards, also had words of praise for the sell-out crowd.

"They were excited tonight," he said. "If they don't think getting loud and all that really works, the first couple of plays you could tell it was to our advantage. I would hate to go into a place where the crowd is excited that way."

The first couple of snaps indeed set the tone.

On Philadelphia's first play from scrimmage, cornerback Doug Evans stepped in front of a Rodney Peete slant pass intended for Chris T. Jones and intercepted it, setting up a field goal.

On Green Bay's next series, Favre, who came out sky-high (as he usually does in big games) and misfired on his first five passes, threw an 11-yard screen pass to halfback Edgar Bennett. That settled Favre and the Packers down.

It was all downhill for the Eagles after that.

Green Bay used a 20-point second quarter, capped by a nine-play, 75-yard drive in the final minute, to build a 30-7 halftime lead.

In the second half, the defense dominated and held the Eagles to 259 total yards while Green Bay piled up 432.

The highlight of the half was the combined sack by Reggie White and Santana Dotson on Peete for a safety that ended the deluge.

Both teams were more than a little amazed by the lopsided win.

"I don't think you ever expect games like

that in this league, but once in a while it happens," Holmgren said. "We're capable of putting up points and we have a fine defense."

The Eagles weren't arguing.

"As you can see, we were thoroughly dominated," Rhodes said somberly. "I figured we'd come in here and be a pretty competitive football team. I really felt that we could be in a position to win a football game tonight but it didn't happen. It hurts to get beat like that."

Eagles' running back Ricky Watters, however, put the correct spin on things for both teams.

"It's just one loss and it's not even our division," he said. "But on national TV is where you can get respect. Monday night, you can get respect off of that. We did not do that tonight. If anything, we lost some."

And for the 2-0 Packers, they gained some.

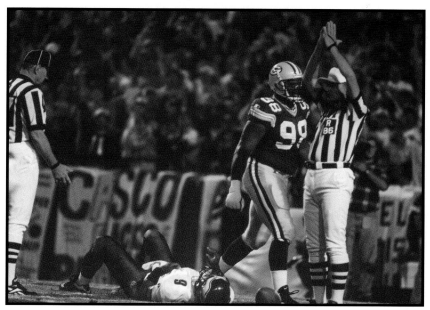

▲ Third–year defensive end Gabe Wilkins started to show the game the Packers coaches always thought he had. Wilkins, seen here exulting over the fallen Rodney Peete, finally played with consistency and fire and allowed the coaching staff to rest Reggie White at key times without the level of play falling off too dramatically. Wilkins had 19 tackles and three quarterback sacks for the season.

▲ A rare and wonderful sight for Packers fans: Backup quarterback Jim McMahon in the game, meaning that the game was out of reach and Brett Favre could rest. McMahon actually played most of the fourth quarter in Green Bay's first three games, all blowouts.

▲ An even rarer sight: second–year back Travis Jervey carrying the ball. Though blessed with great speed, Jervey fumbled four times in 26 carries during the season, and there is nothing that infuriates coach Mike Holmgren more than fumbles. Jervey made up for it by being one of Green Bay's terrors on special teams, finishing with nine tackles while busting up more than a few wedges.

Bob Harlan

Bob Harlan had seen enough.

Since 1971, he'd been in the front office of the Green Bay Packers, and he'd watched with a mixture of sadness and disappointment as the proud franchise descended into mediocrity.

It was now late in 1991 and Harlan, who had been the team's president and CEO for the past two years, could stand it no longer.

The Packers were in the throes of an agonizing 4-12 season under coach Lindy Infante and it was obvious for all to see that something drastic had to be done. So Harlan decided it was time to make the kind of change that gets people to sit up and take notice.

Harlan would buck tradition and hire a real football guy and give him the title and powers of a general manager — the first since Vince Lombardi. And Harlan knew exactly who he wanted, New York Jets personnel director Ron Wolf.

"I remember having lunch with (New York Giants general manager) George Young at the time and telling him how concerned I was about the direction of our franchise," Harlan said. "I told him that I really wanted Ron Wolf and George said, 'Yeah, he'd be good, but you'll never get him out of New York.'"

Harlan knew the right words, though, and he put together the kind of package that Wolf couldn't refuse.

And after Harlan hired Wolf, Wolf hired coach Mike Holmgren and, well, the story more or less takes on a life of its own.

But it starts with Harlan, a quiet but friendly man who doesn't take to the spotlight easily. All he has ever done, he says, is let his football people do the football stuff.

Meanwhile, he has overseen drastic changes in the physical and emotional landscape of the Green Bay Packers.

Since 1989, Lambeau Field has added more than 1,900 club seats and 120 private boxes. Harlan upgraded and expanded the building and training quarters. He spearheaded the construction of the $5 million Don Hutson Center, the Packers new indoor practice facility that is considered one of the finest in the NFL.

He also made the decision in 1994 to end the Packers four-game commitment in Milwaukee, a good-will gesture to the city since 1932.

Citing the need for increased revenue by playing every game in Green Bay, Harlan said the move was necessary to keep the team solvent. Milwaukee season-ticket holders appeared to agree and 94 percent kept their tickets after learning that three games each season would go

The happy Harlan family on Super Bowl Sunday; (L to R) Ann, Kevin, Madeline, Bob, Brian, Michael.

to them.

In fact, almost every move Harlan has made has worked out for the Packers.

It came to full fruition on Super Bowl Sunday when Harlan, Wolf and Holmgren all felt the Vince Lombardi Trophy in their hands.

But as much as that meant to him, Harlan admitted there was an even more special moment.

"From an emotional standpoint, to win the NFC championship, and to have it happen at Lambeau Field, was even better," Harlan said. "Every place I looked, people were jumping and waving. It was such a great reaction. It was just pure joy. That's a scene I'll never forget."

As for the team's long, rich tradition which, until this season, had been as much of a burden as a help, Harlan said there's always a place for it.

"I don't mind talking about the tradition," he said. "That should be treasured. But you have to update it and continue the story. After 30 years, it's time to do something new."

And behind the strong, silent leadership of Harlan, the Packers have done just that.

A Big Charge
September 15: Packers 42, Chargers 10

The Packers took their show outside the NFC for the first time in the season and faced the San Diego Chargers, a Super Bowl team just two years earlier.

Once again, the Packers were scarily in sync, piling up 349 yards on offense and holding San Diego to only 141.

This time, the Packers added a couple of new weapons to their repertoire – big returns from the special teams and defense.

Green Bay never really lost control of this game, taking a 21-3 halftime lead thanks to Favre's touchdown passes to Antonio Freeman and William Henderson and a 10-yard run from Bennett.

The Packers built it to 28-3 in the third quarter when Favre hooked up with Jackson for a touchdown with 1:52 remaining.

San Diego tried to battle back in the fourth quarter when, after a Favre interception, quarterback Stan Humphries threw a touchdown pass to Tony Martin.

On Green Bay's next possession, Bennett fumbled for the first time in four seasons and San Diego took over deep in Packer territory.

Just when it looked like the Chargers were going to make a game of it, safety LeRoy Butler stepped in front of a Humphries throw and returned it 90 yards for the score that broke San Diego's back.

Not even two minutes later, Desmond Howard, the former Heisman Trophy winner who had been a washout in his three previous seasons with Washington and Jacksonville and who only made the Packers roster with a great punt return in preseason, left his own mark.

Howard took a punt, cut up the left sideline and was gone for the 65-yard touchdown that turned a pretty good game into a bona fide rout.

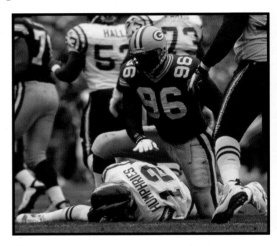

▲ It was a long afternoon for Stan Humphries as he was intercepted twice and sacked five times. This one came courtesy of veteran end Sean Jones, who had two of his five sacks for the season in this game. While his numbers were down, Jones admitted it didn't matter so long as the Packers reached a Super Bowl. He got his wish.

The evidence was growing that these Packers could be something special.

"I think we're pretty good," Butler said. "It's obvious. Everybody's trying to tone it down a little bit. But we're a good team."

Brooks agreed, and said, "This is how we expect to play."

San Diego general manager Bobby Beathard could only shake his head after witnessing the carnage.

"Really not much you can say," he said. "They kicked our butt. They're awfully good."

Safety LeRoy Butler, seen here chasing down Charger Terrell Fletcher, had another Pro Bowl season with 88 tackles, 6.5 sacks and five interceptions. One of his biggest came against San Diego when he intercepted a Stan Humphries pass and returned it 90 yards for the touchdown. It was the first of three interceptions returned for a score by the Packers in 1996.

◀ Tight end Keith Jackson (far left) got off to a monster start in 1996, catching three touchdown passes in the season-opener and another against the Chargers. For the season, he caught 10 touchdown passes and earned his fifth Pro Bowl berth.

◀ Fullback Dorsey Levens ran for 39 yards on nine carries against San Diego. But the best was still to come for the third-year back from Georgia Tech.

◀ Wide receiver Robert Brooks torched the Chargers for eight catches for 108 yards and seemed well on his way to another record-setting season until tragedy struck a month later.

▶ Mark Chmura, Green Bay's Pro Bowl tight end from the year before, saw his numbers drop in 1996, in part due to injury. But while he didn't catch as many passes he took pride in becoming one of the NFL's top blocking tight ends. "My time will come," he said. "I'll catch plenty of passes."

A Big Charge

◀ Reggie White acknowledges the cheers of the Lambeau Field crowd after the Packers' runaway win. He, like Sean Jones, recorded two quarterback sacks on Stan Humphries.

▶ Defensive coordinator Fritz Shurmur offers congratulations to tackle Darius Holland.

▲ Left guard Aaron Taylor proved to be one of the great inspirational stories of the season. Green Bay's top draft pick in 1994, he saw his rookie season ended with a ruptured patellar tendon in his right knee. He battled back and won the starting job in 1995, where he played in all 16 games. But in the first playoff game, he ruptured the patellar tendon in his left knee. Once again, he fought back, returning in 1996 to start in Green Bay's last preseason game. He never missed another game after that.

▲ Adam Timmerman, a seventh-round draft choice from tiny South Dakota State in 1995, had hoped just to land a roster spot with the Packers. By the end of the 1995 season, he was starting in the playoffs in place of the injured Aaron Taylor at left guard. In 1996, he moved over to right guard and was one of the steadiest, and most improved, players on the team.

Back To Earth

September 22: Vikings 30, Packers 21

Coach Mike Holmgren and defensive coordinator Fritz Shurmur look on during pregame warmups in the Metrodome. Holmgren couldn't help but feel trepidation since he had yet to win in Minneapolis as Green Bay's head coach.

THERE IS SOMETHING ABOUT THE METRODOME IN MINNEAPOLIS THAT has turned recent Packers' visits into nightmarish misadventures.

Maybe it's the temperature and humidity inside the place affectionately known as the Humpdome. Maybe it's the artificial turf. Maybe it's when 20,000 visiting Packers fans collide with 40,000 suddenly crazy Vikings fans, the combination is just too volatile for the Packers to handle.

Or maybe it's more basic than that. Maybe it's simply the fact that when the Packers face these guys on that surface, the matchup always favors the smaller, quicker, faster Vikings.

Whatever it is, in his five seasons as Packers coach, Holmgren had yet to beat the Vikings in Minneapolis. And most of the losses had been too bizarre to believe.

On Holmgren's first trip north in 1992, with a playoff berth on the line, the Vikings cruised as journeyman quarterback Sean Salisbury torched the Packers.

The following year, Green Bay had the Vikes beaten until Minnesota quarterback Jim McMahon found an unknown receiver named Eric Guliford for a huge gain that set up Fuad Reveiz's game-winning field goal in the final seconds.

In 1994, Favre was knocked out of the game with a hip injury and youngster Mark Brunell took over at quarterback. Still, Green Bay had a chance to win until a late drive in regulation tied the game and a Reveiz field goal won it in overtime.

But the toughest loss had come just a year earlier, when again Favre was forced from the game, this time with a badly sprained ankle.

Backup Ty Detmer played well for a time before he suffered a thumb injury that sidelined him. That left No. 3 quarterback T.J. Rubley at the control and, amazingly, he appeared to be driving the Packers on a game-winning drive of their own.

To the horror of Holmgren, though, on a third-and-inches play, Rubley audibled out of a quarterback sneak and called for a pass, despite desperate pleas from his linemen.

Rubley's awful lob pass over the middle was intercepted, Minnesota drove the other way and, for the third straight year, Reveiz beat the Packers.

But this time around, it was supposed to be different. At least that's what the Packers were banking on. Green Bay was clearly the better team and would prove it by winning in one of the great NFL snakepits.

Then again...

It proved to be another long afternoon for the Packers as Minnesota this time simply outplayed Green Bay.

"At least this year, I guess you could say we lost it," Packers general manager Ron Wolf said. "No one stepped in and bit us this time. They really won the game."

The swarming Vikings defense held the Packers to 217 total yards and Green Bay's offensive line was hung out to dry to the tune of seven sacks. Just for good measure, the Packers committed four turnovers (three fumbles, one interception) that led to 17 Minnesota points.

"Too many turnovers, too many penalties," a grim Holmgren said afterward.

"That's unacceptable."

But not necessarily unexpected.

The Vikings, after all, knew what few other teams in the NFL did. They knew that when Favre was pressured, he could be forced into occasional mistakes.

"That really disrupts his rhythm," said Vikings linebacker (and one-time Packer) Jeff Brady. "Brett has not played in a lot of those kinds of games and when he does, he has problems. He tries to force things. He tries to do some things instead of maybe taking the sack."

Favre, who completed just 14 of 27 passes for 198 yards and two scores, admitted it wasn't one of his stellar efforts.

"It's part of playing here and we knew that coming in," he said. "It's a pressure football team that you're playing. But you just have to deal with it."

And for a while at least, it seemed Green Bay was dealing with it acceptably.

Favre staked the Packers to a 7-0 first-quarter lead on a pretty 13-yard pass to Robert Brooks. Minnesota then took control, scoring 17 straight points.

But with 9:18 left in the third quarter, Favre hit veteran wide receiver Don Beebe on a short curl-in pattern, which the speedy Beebe fashioned into an 80-yard touchdown, cutting the Vikes' lead to 17-14.

Five minutes later, the defense did its part as middle linebacker George Koonce stepped in front of a Warren Moon pass and rumbled 75 yards down the left sideline for a touchdown.

Yet it wouldn't last. It never does for the Packers here.

With barely four minutes left in the game, Vikings tailback Robert Smith slipped off right guard and scored nearly untouched to give Minnesota a 24-21 lead.

A pair of field goals in the final two minutes sealed Green Bay's fate and sent the Packers to their first loss of the season.

"I don't know anybody in this room who thought we were going to go 16-0," Favre said. "We'll just go on and play from here. We'll have forgotten this one by tomorrow."

Well, by Tuesday, tops.

▲ Gilbert Brown, Green Bay's 325-pound nose tackle, had a career season with 52 tackles. But where Brown, who ironically was cut three years earlier by Minnesota, was at his best was stopping teams from running up the middle. It got to the point that by late in the season teams didn't even bother running the ball any more.

▲ Reggie White swoops in to scoop up a Warren Moon fumble forced by the blitzing LeRoy Butler (36). ▲

▲ Linebacker Wayne Simmons closes in on Minnesota receiver Cris Carter. Simmons, the Packers top draft pick from 1993, had his best season in 1996 with 67 tackles and an interception.

▶ LeRoy Butler (left) and Mike Prior (right) congratulate safety Eugene Robinson after he makes his first-ever interception as a Packer. The pick led to Green Bay's first touchdown of the game. Robinson led the Packers with six interceptions during the regular season and is the NFL's all-time leading active interceptor with 48.

◄ Defensive end Sean Jones and tackle Santana Dotson converge on Minnesota quarterback Warren Moon in the end zone. Moon was sacked twice and threw two interceptions.

◄ Desmond Howard (left) and Antonio Freeman (right) congratulate Don Beebe after his 80-yard scoring play. Beebe turned a five-yard curl-in into a touchdown that got the Packers back into the game. In a month, Beebe's role would grow dramatically.

▲ Linebacker George Koonce keeps a death grip on the ball after scoring on a 75-yard interception return. For the five-year veteran, it was his first touchdown of any kind since high school. A refugee from the old World League, Koonce caught on with the Packers and has been a stalwart. This season, he moved from right outside linebacker to middle linebacker and led the team in tackles. But his season ended in the playoffs when he injured a knee against San Francisco.

◄ Vikings' tailback Robert Smith slips away from cornerback Doug Evans (33) and linebacker George Koonce and runs 37 yards for a touchdown that put Minnesota on top to stay in the fourth quarter. The defeat was Green Bay's fifth straight at the Metrodome and handed the Packers their first loss of the season.

Back To Earth

Kingdome Come
September 29: Packers 31, Seahawks 10

Eugene Robinson spent his first 11 pro seasons as a Seattle Seahawk and remains one of the franchise's most popular players. He tried to downplay the return home but he admitted it was tough, especially when he received a standing ovation from the Kingdome crowd. But that changed quickly when he intercepted a Rick Mirer pass and returned it 39 yards to set up a Packers touchdown.

HERE IS LITTLE THAT ANNOYS HOLMGREN MORE THAN WHEN HIS TEAM'S record on artificial turf comes up in conversation.

In Holmgren's first four seasons, the Packers were 5-16 on the fake stuff and the record wasn't helped any by Green Bay's performance the week before in Minneapolis.

Holmgren's argument: Six of those losses came at the hands of the powerful Cowboys and four others were in the Metrodome.

So, taking that into the account, the record wasn't really all that bad.

Nonetheless, the Packers realized if they were going to turn their season back in the proper direction, they'd have to do it on the plastic carpet of Seattle's cavernous Kingdome.

Fortunately for the Packers, they were playing a young Seattle team still trying to find its own identity and not entirely sure where to look.

In this one, the Green Bay defense was superb, intercepting befuddled Seahawks quarterback Rick Mirer four times, and the offense was just functional enough as Green Bay righted the ship with an easy win.

"Listen, I want that to be the headline in every paper in the country: 'Holmgren does it on turf,'" Holmgren said, only half-joking. "Heck, we've lost to Minnesota and Dallas because we weren't as good (as they were). The turf had very little to do with that in those games. That really has skewed my won-loss record. But I still want those headlines."

The coach would have to share them with a Green Bay defense that showed enticing glimpses of just how dominating it would become as the season progressed.

Safety Eugene Robinson, a Seahawks icon for 11 seasons, got the ball rolling in the opening quarter when he tricked Mirer into throwing a corner pattern when his receiver was running a post. As a result,

Robinson was all by himself to make an interception he returned 39 yards to set up one Green Bay touchdown.

Needless to say, the week before this game, the affable, quotable, intelligent Robinson was the center of some serious media attention. After all, he'd spent his entire career with the Seahawks and had become a living legend in the Northwest. He still owned a home there, he still did charity work there, he still loved it there.

But after 11 seasons, it became impossible for him to work there any longer. Salary cap woes forced the Seahawks to deal him to the Packers on June 27 for defensive end Matt LaBounty.

"It's one of the toughest things I ever had to do," Seattle coach Dennis Erickson said. "Not only is Eugene still a great player, but he's a great man."

Seattle's loss was Green Bay's gain and the veteran Robinson helped steady a young but talented secondary that featured cornerbacks Craig Newsome (second year) and Doug Evans (fourth year). Robinson also gave a new lease on life to another veteran safety, LeRoy Butler, who had been to the Pro Bowl three years earlier but had not returned.

"He's just taken me under his wing," Evans said of Robinson. "From the start of training camp, he was always working with us to make us better."

Robinson alternately relished and dreaded going back to Seattle for this game.

"It's just another game on the schedule for me," he said, though few believed him. "I understand why the Seahawks did what they did. It was a business decision and I know that. But now I'm a Green Bay Packer and I'm going to do everything I can to help this team win."

And in Seattle, Robinson's young mates rose up with him.

Evans, perhaps the most improved defender on the team, picked off a Mirer toss and ran it back 63 yards, setting up another touchdown.

Defensive tackle Santana Dotson got into the act as well, scooping up a fumble and nearly scoring, as did the inimitable Reggie White, who rumbled 46 yards with an interception to set up a field goal.

Those five turnovers led to 24 Green Bay points.

"All of us (on defense) want to be the guy that wins the game for us," Evans said.

Favre, meanwhile, completed 20 of 34 passes for 209 yards. Included in that flurry were four touchdown throws, two to emerging star Antonio Freeman.

Freeman, a second-year player from Virginia

▲ Bernardo Harris, a backup linebacker, is also one of the Packers' special team whizzes. Here, he prepares to down a punt deep in Seattle territory.

▶ Wayne Simmons roars in to separate quarterback Rick Mirer from the ball. It was a big-time comeback for the defense after the heartbreak in Minnesota. Against the Seahawks, the defense allowed 329 yards but forced five turnovers, including this fumble that Santana Dotson (71) picked up.

Tech whom several teams shied away from because of a perceived reluctance to catch balls over the middle, blossomed against the Seahawks when flanker Robert Brooks went down with a concussion on the game's first play.

Still annoyed at being a third-round draft pick the year before, Freeman stepped in and caught seven passes for 108 yards, both career highs.

"I was Robert's primary backup last year," said Freeman, who beat out Anthony Morgan for the split end job opposite Brooks but was forced to switch sides with Brooks' injury. "It's like second nature to me. I think that's one of the things I bring to the table."

Even Holmgren was impressed with Freeman's performance. Eventually, that is.

"He was much better in the second half," Holmgren said. "He did a couple of things in the first half that I didn't like and we chatted about it at halftime. He's young and he'll make a lot of young mistakes. I told him, 'I just don't have time for that mistake and neither do you, so let's get it going.' And he really responded."

The most impressive play, and one that showed the burgeoning chemistry between Favre and Freeman, came early in the fourth quarter with Green Bay comfortably ahead 24-10.

On third-and-goal from the Seattle 4-yard line, Favre was flushed from the pocket and rolled left. He thought about running the ball in, but two Seahawks were waiting for him.

Then at the last second, Favre saw Freeman break open in the middle of the end zone. Brett flipped a pass underhanded and Freeman made a diving catch.

"Incredible," Seahawks cornerback Corey Harris said with a resigned shake of his head.

Incredible, perhaps, but a result that was proving less and less surprising to Packer followers.

Green Bay gained 344 total yards to Seattle's 329. But the Packers were never really threatened.

For the Packers, the month of September was a solid one in which they went 4-1. They had faced two playoff teams in Philadelphia and San Diego and whipped them both by a combined score of 81-23. They also had played three road games and come away 2-1, an impressive beginning for a team that had struggled away from Lambeau under Holmgren.

With a rugged October looming, the Packers were off to a good start. But that's all it was — a start.

◀ It was not the best of days for Rick Mirer, who besides throwing four interceptions, was sacked once. Gabe Wilkins lets Mirer know he's around on this play.

▼ After Green Bay's easy win, three of the NFL's best defensive players stop to chat: Packers Sean Jones and Reggie White and Seattle tackle Cortez Kennedy.

Chapter 3

Bearly A Sweat

October 6: Packers 37, Bears 6

ACKERS-BEARS. LOMBARDI-HALAS. BUTKUS-NITSCHKE. LUCKMAN-Canadeo.

There aren't many rivalries in sports that stir the blood like the Chicago Bears against the Green Bay Packers.

They are ancient rivals, forged in the fledgling days of the NFL. They represent two very different cities, yet they also represent two very similar ideals.

Both franchises have known their share of glory and torment. Both have been to the top of the mountain and into the deepest valley.

But after so many years, after so many games, after so many players have come and gone, the rivalry remains as nasty and wonderful as ever.

It is coming under attack, however, thanks mostly to the cool efficiency of Holmgren and his team and the struggling of the Bears under coach Dave Wannstedt.

This new era really started four years ago when the Bears were still ruled by Mike Ditka.

Back then, an upstart bunch of Packers, led by some wild-armed kid at quarterback named Favre, engineered an impressive 17-3 win over Chicago at Soldier Field.

Since then, it has been almost all Packers.

In 1994, the Packers crushed the Bears twice by a combined score of 73-9. The next year, the Packers beat the Bears twice more, 27-24 in Chicago and 35-28 at Lambeau when Favre, on a badly sprained and heavily taped ankle, threw five touchdown passes.

But here was a new season, a new chance for the Bears to even the score and jump-start a rivalry that was in danger of fading away.

It seemed early on that it might happen, too, when Bears safety Marty Carter intercepted a Brett Favre pass and Chicago struck off on a drive that resulted in a quick 3-0 lead.

Things wouldn't go quite that smoothly for the Bears the rest of the way.

Driving deep in Packers territory with momentum still on his side, Chicago quarterback Dave Krieg lofted a pass into the back of the end zone that was intercepted by Wayne Simmons.

That would mark the beginning of the end for the Bears, keeping Green Bay on its recent roll in this series.

Left guard Aaron Taylor leads halfback Edgar Bennett through a hole against the Chicago Bears.

▶ **Though he's off to the races after making this catch, Robert Brooks' season would end the following week after he sustained a serious knee injury against the 49ers. Brooks, who caught six passes for 68 yards and a touchdown against Chicago, ended the year with 23 receptions and four touchdowns.**

▶ It was a long strange, season for Gary Brown. The affable third-year player from Georgia Tech, fondly referred to as "Bubblin' Bertha," began the season as Green Bay's starting left tackle. But after four games, he lost his job to rookie John Michels, then reclaimed it again against the Bears. But after that, he saw only spot duty and, in fact, was inactive the final 11 games of the season.

▶ Defensive tackle Santana Dotson was everything that was advertised, and more, for the Packers. Signed as a free-agent from Tampa Bay when several other prospects fell through, Dotson had a superb season with 38 tackles, 5.5 sacks and six passes defensed.

After going scoreless in first quarter, the Packers erupted against the flagging Bears defense. It started when Favre scrambled left and found Brooks in the back of the end zone for a 18-yard touchdown with 9:27 left in the half.

The onslaught continued when Favre hit tight end Keith Jackson for a 2-yard score that boosted the lead to 14-3.

Then came the back-breaker for the Bears.

In the waning moments of the half, Krieg threw an awful pass that was intercepted by Evans and taken back to the 50. After two incompletions, the Packers had time for one more play. Favre rolled right and with defensive end Alonzo Spellman bearing down on him, launched a Hail Mary pass into the crowded end zone.

Freeman yanked safety Mark Carrier out of the way, leaped into the crowd and made the catch that stunned the Bears and gave Green Bay a 20-3 halftime lead.

Freeman admitted he may not have played exactly fair in that situation.

"I was making room to make the catch," he said.

Carrier's version: "We weren't expecting the Hail Mary so we weren't in our Hail Mary defense. I thought maybe they'd run something down the middle of the field. I don't want to say we weren't prepared, we had it. We had the players in the game but we weren't expecting it."

Shocked by the late fireworks, the Bears put up little defense in the second half.

Chicago did close to within 20-6 early in the third quarter, but on the following kickoff, Beebe skipped between two blockers and scampered 90 yards for the touchdown that put the game out of reach.

Freeman wasn't quite done, though.

With 4:07 left in the third quarter and the Packers on the Chicago 35, Favre heaved a pass in Freeman's general vicinity. Freeman leaped and twisted and contorted himself to get in front of safety Kevin Miniefield and made a spectacular grab for the touchdown.

It was Freeman's answer to Holmgren who, for the third straight game, barked at the wide receiver at halftime for mistakes he'd made in the first half.

"We had our normal ritual in the first half where I had to jump him for something," Holmgren said. "Then, all of a sudden, he gets mad at me and starts playing. So that's good. He was spectacular. Just spectacular."

Freeman admitted the coach was on him again.

"He gets his word in every game and it has an effect on me in some kind of way," Freeman said. "It's just ironic that I come out and play well."

Fellow wide receiver Robert Brooks, on the other hand, took exception to post-game questions about Freeman's sudden jump into the limelight.

"What emergence?" Brooks said. "He's already been here. I'm really getting tired of people saying he's emerging. He's no surprise to me."

The victory over the Bears also marked another stellar performance by Favre, who completed 18 of 27 passes for 246 yards and four touchdowns. That gave him 20 touchdown throws in his first six games, which pro-

▲ Linebacker Wayne Simmons made perhaps the key play of the game against the Bears when he intercepted a Dave Krieg pass in the end zone that snuffed out Chicago's first legitimate drive. It was never really a game after that.

◄ He never got the credit he deserved this season, but defensive line coach Larry Brooks used just the right mix of enthusiasm, ego-stroking and butt-kicking to get the point across. "He played the game," end Reggie White said. "And because he did, you know he knows what he's talking about."

jected out to an NFL-record 48 over an entire season.

"It's flattering to hear all the things that are said," Favre responded. "But the bottom line is I want to win. If the numbers come with it, great. But I'd much rather get to the Super Bowl."

For the game, Green Bay totally dominated the Bears, outgaining them in total yardage, 348-243, and extended the Packers' winning streak over Chicago to five straight.

"We love dominating teams," safety LeRoy Butler said. "I think the Bears caught a team that was very hot, very disciplined, just a dominating team."

The Bears certainly were in no position to argue.

◀ Desmond Howard (right) and Doug Evans congratulate Antonio Freeman after he made a diving touchdown catch that gave Green Bay a 34-6 cushion.

▶ A familiar sight in 1996: Brett Favre celebrating a touchdown pass to tight end Keith Jackson. In this game, Favre threw a nine-yard strike to Jackson, his sixth touchdown reception of the young season, that gave the Packers a 14-3 second-quarter lead.

Ron Wolf

There are times Ron Wolf gets a look on his face that can only be described as venomous bemusement.

When challenged on a personnel move or queried about a draft pick gone south, he'll get a little half-smile on his face and he'll roll his eyes and he'll prepare to speak, then stop while he searches for the proper word.

Wolf used that look a lot in his first few seasons as the Green Bay Packers general manager. He knew when he was hired on Nov. 28, 1991, that the strongest house was built with a quality foundation, and it would take time for that foundation to settle.

This much was certain: Wolf, who was given complete control of the football operations, would do things his way and, he hoped, the right way.

"I had eight names on my list of people I wanted for this job and Ron Wolf's name was at the top," team president Bob Harlan said. "I figured anybody who worked 25 years for Al Davis had to be dedicated and talented or he wouldn't have been there. He'd been to a Super Bowl and won it and that was important."

Wolf wasted no time in putting his mark on the Packers, firing head coach Lindy Infante at the end of the 1991 season and going full-bore at hiring Mike Holmgren.

Holmgren, who was offensive coordinator of the San Francisco 49ers, was the hottest head-coaching prospect in football. And after interviewing with three other teams, he signed on with the Packers.

Since then, Wolf and Holmgren have worked in an atmosphere as close to harmony as you can have in the fractious world of pro football.

"Ron made it very clear to me early on that he did not want to coach the football team," Holmgren said. "I told him I appreciated that."

Wolf went out and traded a No. 1 draft pick to the Atlanta Falcons for Brett Favre. He lured high-priced free agent Reggie White to Green Bay. He drafted the likes of Mark Chmura, Robert Brooks, Antonio Freeman, Dorsey Levens and Wayne Simmons. He plucked Gilbert Brown off waivers, signed Desmond Howard when no one else wanted him and took a chance on Andre Rison when other teams figured he was a pariah.

Wolf's made his share of mistakes, too, and no one is more willing to own up to them.

Wolf made cornerback Terrell Buckley a first-round pick in 1992 and regretted it almost immediately. He also let tight end Jackie Harris and linebackers Bryce Paup and Tony Bennett get away in free agency.

But since the 1993 draft, 24 picks are still with the team, including nine starters.

"The Packers are a great story," Wolf said. "They have a great tradition. To finally achieve this, to take advantage of that history, to play in the best stadium and in front of the best fans in the NFL because they supported this team for 29 years when it did diddly, it's a remarkable story."

A story Wolf had a large hand in writing.

Ron Wolf (middle) with sons Eliot (left) and Jonathan.

Jacked Up

October 14: Packers 23, 49ers 20 (OT)

ASK PACKERS FIELD GOAL KICKER CHRIS JACKE AND HE'LL SAY HE'D rather kick extra points than field goals any day of the week.

The Packer with the longest tenure (eight years) is no fan of suspense, even though his career in Green Bay began just that way with several game-winning kicks during his rookie season in 1989.

In fact, since Mike Holmgren took over as head coach in 1992, Jacke had kicked just one game-winner – against New Orleans in the Superdome in '93.

All that changed on this strange, wonderful, painful, exhilarating, stressful Monday night at Lambeau Field.

It was pretty simple, really.

The Packers were 5-1, but who had they played?

They'd beaten up three mediocre teams in Tampa Bay, Seattle and Chicago. They'd handled two teams that were supposed to be contenders in Philadelphia and San Diego, but the verdict was really still out on them.

And their toughest test, in Minneapolis against the Vikings, had been a failure.

So into town strode the big, bad San Francisco 49ers, still the kings of the NFC West and still smarting from a 27-17 loss to the Packers the previous January in the NFC playoffs. That was a game no one in the Bay Area could believe nearly a year

after the fact.

The Packers knew this would be a test, not only on the football field, but in their minds as well. Deep down, way deep down, the Packers felt they could compete with the Niners. They knew they had the personnel, the scheme, the ability to match up well with San Francisco.

But there was also that uncertainty. Had the Packers been lucky the previous January? Had the 49ers not taken them seriously? Had the Packers simply played the kind of game that appears once every three seasons?

This would be a chance for the Packers to show they really belonged with the big boys.

The 49ers came in at less than full strength, most notably without quarterback Steve Young, who was sidelined with a hamstring injury. In his place stood Elvis Grbac, a solid backup who was itching to prove he could assume the role from Young and possibly become the heir as starting quarterback.

The Packers didn't care if Mickey Mouse was under center, they knew a win over San Francisco on the national stage would go a long way toward legitimizing them this season.

And it became clear that if that was going to happen, the Packers would have to earn it.

On Green Bay's first offensive play, wide receiver Robert Brooks locked up with Niners cornerback Tyronne Drakeford and collapsed in a heap on the ground.

The bigggest game of the Packers' season to date started ominously when, on the first play, Robert Brooks locked up with cornerback Tyronne Drakeford and tore the anterior cruciate and patellar tendon in his right knee. Don Beebe took his place and the rest, as they say, is history.

The diagnosis was bad: a torn anterior cruciate and a ruptured patellar tendon, perhaps the worst knee injury possible.

Brooks, Green Bay's big-play receiver and its most experienced, obviously done – not just for the game, but the entire season – and the Packers struggled to adapt.

"I don't think I've ever felt so bad for a player who got hurt in a game," said fellow wideout Don Beebe. "It really hurts to see him miss the rest of the season. But he knows he'll be back. Guys like Robert Brooks always come back."

Freeman moved into Brooks' flanker spot once again and Beebe, who barely made the roster after a so-so training camp, slid into Freeman's slot at split end.

The results were remarkable.

The Packers seemed to be taking control early, moving on the 49ers defense, which was ranked second in the NFL.

But in the so-called "red zone" – from the opponent's 20-yard-line to the goal line – the Packers uncharacteristically fizzled.

Jacke field goals of 30 and 25 yards in the first quarter did stake Green Bay to a 6-0 lead.

Clearly, though, that wouldn't be nearly enough.

Momentum swung midway through the second quarter, when the Packers failed to convert on fourth-and-five from the San Francisco 34.

The 49ers turned it the other way, drove 36 yards and got a Jeff Wilkins field goal out of it.

On its next possession, San Francisco moved

Left tackle Gary Brown (left) and right tackle Earl Dotson team up to stop 49ers' defensive tackle Bryant Young.

After making a huge third-down reception, Don Beebe shows some rare emotion on the field. Beebe stepped in for the fallen Brooks and had the game of his life: 11 catches for 220 yards, which was third-highest in club history.

58 yards in eight plays and scored when Grbac threw a 7-yard touchdown pass to Jerry Rice with 2:20 left in the half.

Things got worse for the Packers as Niners defensive end Dana Stubblefield intercepted a Favre pass and returned it 15 yards to the Green Bay 28. Five plays later, Rice scored on another Grbac pass and San Francisco held a comfortable 17-6 cushion.

And then the game really got interesting.

In the third quarter, the Packers finally got something going, though they needed more than a little help from the officials.

Midway through the quarter, Beebe made a sliding catch near the Green Bay sideline at the 49ers' 30. Though it appeared Niners cornerback Marquez Pope touched Beebe to end the play, Beebe popped up and ran the rest of the way.

After a lengthy conference, the officials ruled no one had touched Beebe (though replays clearly showed Pope did) and Beebe was credited with a 59-yard touchdown that gave the Packers badly needed breath.

◄ Chris Jacke (arms raised) and holder Craig Hentrich celebrate Jacke's game-winning 53-yard field goal in overtime that beat the 49ers. Jacke made five field goals that night, including a 31-yarder in the final seconds of regulation that sent the game into overtime.

"It was definitely a catch," Beebe said diplomatically. "Whether he touched me or not, I wasn't sure. But I was taught to keep running until the whistle blows and I did not hear the whistle blow."

And there was the break the Packers were seeking.

Trailing 17-12, the Packers went for two points after the touchdown and Favre threw short to Bennett, who dove into the end zone. Again, replays showed Bennett's knee was down before he reached the end zone, but the officials let the conversion stand and the Packers were back in it, 17-14.

Green Bay tied the game with 3:52 left in regulation on Jacke's third field goal, a 35-yarder.

That's when the game got really wild.

Backed deep in their own territory, Favre and rookie wide receiver Derrick Mayes miscommunicated on a pattern and Pope came up with an interception at the Packers' 12.

"After I threw the interception, I thought, 'Well, that's it,' " Favre said.

But curiously, San Francisco coach George Seifert chose not to take a shot into the end zone from such great field position.

Instead, three running plays netted just two yards and Wilkins came on to boot what appeared to be the game-winning 28-yard field goal.

"I wish I had that to do over again," Seifert said of his ultra-conservative strategy.

With still nearly two minutes to play, Favre had plenty of time to rally the Packers.

Favre got some help from 49ers nickel back Steve Israel, who was called for a hands-to-the-face penalty on Freeman. When Israel bumped an official while protesting the call, he was tossed from the game and given an additional 15-yard unsportsmanlike conduct penalty, putting the ball on the 49ers' 45.

Eventually, the Packers moved to the Niners 14 before Jacke was called on to nail the game-tying field goal with 12 seconds left.

San Francisco won the coin toss in overtime but could do nothing, thanks in part to a dropped pass by wide receiver J.J. Stokes that would have kept a drive alive.

Green Bay took over and sparked by a huge 13-yard pass to Beebe on third-and-seven from the Packers' 47, Jacke got his chance to be a reluctant hero.

"I hate situations like that," he said. "There's no way I wanted to be in that situation."

But he had no choice. And neither did

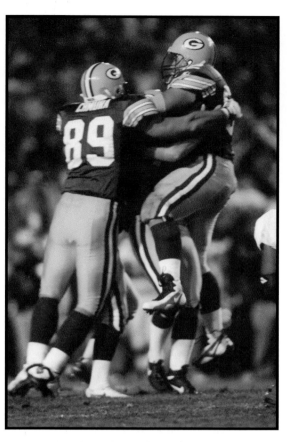

Actually, Jacke never got to see the kick sail through the uprights after he was mobbed by teammates like Mark Chmura (89) and center Frank Winters.

Packers team aid, Father John Blaha, presents Jacke with the game ball afterward.

▲ Good friends Brett Favre and Chmura celebrate the 23-20 win. Favre threw a club-record 61 passes, completing 28, for 395 yards. He also threw one touchdown, two interceptions and was sacked twice. "I never want to play another game like that," Favre said. "It was brutal."

▲ Coach Mike Holmgren, general manager Ron Wolf and Brett Favre reflect on the remarkable game just concluded.

Holmgren, who didn't hesitate a second on deciding whether to try a 53-yarder.

"There was no discussion at all," said punter and holder Craig Hentrich. "It was a no-brainer."

Frank Winters' snap from center was perfect, as was Hentrich's hold. And Jacke's kick sailed over the crossbar with plenty to spare.

"I knew as soon as I kicked it that it was good," said Jacke, who never saw the result because he was mobbed by his teammates. "It's one of the better balls I've kicked in a long time."

Jacke's boomer also brought to a conclusion one of the more memorable games in recent Packers history.

Favre attempted a club-record 61 passes and completed 28 for 395 yards. Meanwhile, Beebe, subbing for the fallen Brooks, caught 11 passes (tying him for fourth-best in Packers history) for 220 yards (third best).

"That little guy can play, can't he?" Holmgren marveled.

The Packers piled up 446 total yards to San Francisco's 253. And though beforehand the Packers had tried to convince themselves this was just another game in a long season, the truth came out.

"I got kind of emotional afterward because it's probably one of the biggest wins of my career," defensive end Reggie White said.

And from Favre: "That was one hell of a ballgame."

Mike Holmgren

Beneath his cool, Scandinavian exterior, Mike Holmgren was irritated.

All Super Bowl week, Holmgren had been the other coach, the new guy, the one who wouldn't know how to handle the pressure and the hype and the scrutiny of the world's biggest football game.

Throughout the week, he had watched as his New England Patriots counterpart, the curmudgeonly Bill Parcells, stole the thunder. First there was the story of how Parcells was coaching his final game with the Patriots. Then came the story about how no coach was better with two weeks to prepare for an opponent than Parcells.

Though Holmgren never lost his accommodating demeanor with the national press, inside he was far from pleased with the "comparisons".

"I guess I'm kind of the coaching underdog here," he would say.

But he knew otherwise.

"I think coach Holmgren took it personally, a slap in the face," safety LeRoy Butler said. "He wanted to say, 'I'm a great coach, too.'

"Parcells said to (the Patriots), he'll show them how to win the game. 'The difference,' coach Holmgren said, 'is that I've already shown you guys how to win. Go do it.' That's the difference."

Indeed, if points were awarded for coaching the Super Bowl, the big Swede from California would have won in a landslide.

Already acknowledged as one of the best game-day coaches in the league, Holmgren showed in the Super Bowl that he could put the distractions aside and coach a solid game. Properly prepared, the Packers played in control all day, committing just three penalties and never getting rattled, even when they fell behind in the first quarter.

But the Super Bowl was just a microcosm of what Holmgren did all season, adjusting on the fly, making necessary changes, running the team with a velvet sledgehammer.

"I think I've gotten better each year in this job," said Holmgren, whose 58 wins in five seasons places him third all-time in club history behind two icons — Curly Lambeau (212) and Vince Lombardi (98). "I've still got a long way to go, though. But I've learned to delegate more, I've learned to trust a little bit more."

This season, Holmgren probably did his best job ever. He started by forbidding Super Bowl talk during the regular season, and it was only after the NFC title game that he was ready to use what he called "the S word."

And though the Packers were favored to win the Super Bowl as early as training camp,

Mike Holmgren and wife Kathy celebrate the Super Bowl victory.

Holmgren managed to keep them focused on the simple but accurate axiom of one game at a time.

Even during games, he was able to make adjustments.

When Robert Brooks was lost for the season with a knee injury early against the 49ers, Holmgren slipped Don Beebe into the role and Beebe had a career game as Green Bay won.

Against Tampa Bay, when Antonio Freeman broke his arm, Holmgren again made the necessary adjustments and the Packers moved along.

Stoic, usually unflappable, he has brought that same attitude to his team.

The only exception in Holmgren's world is Brett Favre, his mercurial quarterback.

The two always have been like fire and ice, and early in their relationship they did not get along. But as Holmgren learned about Favre and vice versa, a mutual respect developed that has helped carry Favre to the top of the league.

"He still does things on the field that...challenge me," Holmgren said with a smile.

For the Packers, winning Super Bowl XXXI was as much for their head coach as it was for them. Because, finally, they now believe he'll get the respect he's deserved but never really received.

"He's still an underrated coach," fullback William Henderson said. "He's brought a team together that's done a lot and will continue to do a lot if we give him the chance."

Hanging On

October 27: Packers 13, Buccaneers 7

T HESE ARE THE KINDS OF GAMES MIKE HOLMGREN HATES.

Always has. Always will.

It was the type of game the Packers know they should win easily but rarely do. The kind that should be a mismatch but isn't. The kind of game that shouldn't signal danger, but does.

The Packers had manhandled the Buccaneers, 34-3, in the season-opener Sept. 1. Besides, now the Packers were playing at home where they were practically invincible.

But there were danger signs as well. Green Bay was coming off its bye week, which followed an emotional and draining win over the 49ers before that.

Besides that, with the loss of Brooks, the Packers offense was struggling.

Also, the Bucs, under new head coach Tony Dungy, clearly were playing better since the last time Green Bay had seen them.

So all in all, Holmgren had a bad feeling about this one. And as it turned out, he had good reason to be concerned.

The Packers were not pretty and they were not particularly effective against Tampa Bay, gaining just 298 total yards. All they did was win.

"I had some concerns about this game," said Holmgren, referring to the fact that Green Bay was a 17-point favorite. "No one should be favored in this league by as many points as we were favored by. But we won the game and I'm just tickled pink that we did."

"It was a win," echoed Favre. "And we're 7-1."

The Packers played efficiently enough, turning a Reggie White blocked punt into a first quarter Jacke field goal. In the second quarter, fullback Dorsey Levens blasted off left tackle for a one-yard touchdown run and, with 59 seconds remaining in the half, Jacke added a 48-yard field goal to give Green Bay a 13-0 lead.

But that was it. The Packers couldn't score the rest of the afternoon.

Meanwhile, Tampa Bay scrapped back, closing to within six points in the fourth quarter when quarterback Trent Dilfer threw an 11-yard touchdown pass to tight end Dave Moore.

Suddenly, a game that should have been a walkover was too close for comfort.

Tampa Bay even had one last chance to pull off the upset, but any hopes of a late game-winning drive were snuffed out when linebacker Brian Williams and safety LeRoy Butler sacked Dilfer on his own 35 in the final seconds.

"This was huge," Holmgren said. "We might not have won that game a couple or three years ago."

The victory did not come without cost, however.

Antonio Freeman, who just the game before had taken over for the injured Robert Brooks, dived for an underthrown Favre pass with 6:15 left in the first quarter. As he sailed toward the ground, Freeman extended his left arm and it hit the knee of Bucs' safety Melvin Johnson.

The collision snapped Freeman's ulnar

Veteran left tackle Ken Ruettgers, who had been sidelined all season with a knee injury, saw his first action of the season against Tampa Bay. He gamely tried to play on the leg for a month but finally retired Nov. 19.

► Safety LeRoy Butler had perhaps his best game of the season in the rematch with Tampa Bay as he finished with a season-high 11 tackles and added 1.5 sacks.

Defensive end Reggie White roars in to sack Bucs' quarterback Trent Dilfer.

▼ Nose tackle Gilbert Brown is more than a run-stopper. Here, he gets his mitts in the air to try and disrupt a Dilfer pass.

bone, sidelining him for what doctors said would be four to six weeks.

"It could have been worse," Freeman said. "At least I'm not out for the season. Now I'll be back when it's for all the marbles."

Freeman admitted, though, that the injury couldn't have come at a worse time for him or the Packers.

"I'm still getting over it," he said. "It was an opportunity for me to go out and establish myself as a legitimate receiver in this league and I was definitely looking forward to it. This will set me back a little, but I'll be back."

Still, with the toughest part of the schedule looming, it was a blow the Packers could not afford.

▶ Though he'd be known this season for his special teams prowess, Desmond Howard also figured in the offense. And with the absence of Robert Brooks and Antonio Freeman, who broke an arm in this game, Howard came on to catch a season-high five passes for 30 yards.

Desmond Howard

He was gone.

Quite simply, Desmond Howard was gone. Cut. Released.

Howard had signed with the Green Bay Packers just before training camp as a free agent, when the Jacksonville Jaguars decided they no longer needed him. And since his phone wasn't exactly ringing off the hook, Howard went to the Packers.

But he'd done nothing in camp. Literally.

A hip pointer had sidelined him through the first two preseason games and he'd done no significant practicing, so the coaching staff really had no idea what he could accomplish. And they didn't have time to find out.

"If we'd only played two preseason games, he wouldn't have made the team," coach Mike Holmgren said bluntly.

Fortunately for Howard and the Packers, the preseason went a little longer. To August 11, specifically, when Green Bay played Pittsburgh in its last home preseason game before the real thing began.

In that game, Howard, who still wasn't fully recovered from his injury but knew his time was running out, took a punt back 77 yards for a touchdown to secure a roster spot.

"I knew if I got a chance to prove myself, I'd come through," Howard said.

He came through all the way to being named MVP of the Super Bowl and it may be one of the NFL's all-time great comeback stories.

It started in 1992 when the reigning Heisman Trophy winner from the University of Michigan was taken as the fourth pick overall by the defending Super Bowl champion Washington Redskins. But in three seasons there, he caught just 66 passes and, surprisingly, returned only 10 punts.

Howard was claimed by Jacksonville in the expansion draft, but he caught just 26 passes and averaged 10.3 yards on 24 punt returns in 1995.

Then on July 11, an intrigued Ron Wolf, who would have drafted Howard in 1992 if Washington hadn't moved up, signed him.

As deep as the Packers were at wide receiver, Wolf knew Howard's strength would be on special teams, especially punt returns, which was a weak area.

Howard started quickly by averaging 14 yards on three returns in the opener against Tampa Bay. But it was two weeks later, against San Diego, where Howard offered evidence of how important he'd be to the Packers as he returned a punt 65 yards for a touchdown.

He stayed consistent all season, never fumbling a kick and rarely making a bad decision.

Then came Howard's phenomenal streak at

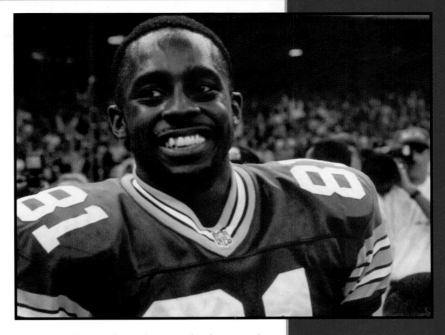

season's end. First, he took a punt back 75 yards to break open a game against the Chicago Bears. Two weeks after that, he went back 92 yards against Detroit, shattering the league record for punt return yardage in a season along the way. In the season finale against Minnesota, he had 47- and 37-yard returns.

"We began kidding him during the week," said special teamer Chris Hayes. "We'd say, 'Des, you better take two back this week.' He's just the best punt returner I've ever seen. He can make guys miss so easily and then you can't catch him."

Then came Howard's playoff wizardry.

On a sloppy track against San Francisco, he hauled a punt return 71 yards for a touchdown, and five minutes later took another back 46 yards to set up another score.

The following week against Carolina, he returned a kickoff 49 yards.

Desmond saved his best for last.

In the Super Bowl, he returned the game's first punt 32 yards, setting up Green Bay's first score. In the second quarter, he returned another 34 yards, leading to a Packer field goal.

But it was his 99-yard kickoff return for a touchdown in the third quarter, the longest in Super Bowl history, that turned the tide for good.

Howard's 244 return yards also set a Super Bowl record and earned him the game's MVP award, the first time a special teams player earned the honor.

"I always said the cream rises to the top," Howard said. "You can only keep talent down for so long. This was no renaissance. You have to be dead for that. And I wasn't dead."

Chapter 4
Systematic
November 3: Packers 28, Lions 18

N THE END, IT COMES DOWN TO THE SYSTEM.

It has always been that way for Mike Holmgren. The players may change, but the system never does.

It can't, for that is what Holmgren relies on to make sense out of a game that relies on little logic. He has a simple, unquestioning, uncomplicated faith.

"I'm confident in what we do," Holmgren said. "I believe in the system."

You would not call it a particularly complicated creed that Holmgren and his Packers live by. But it must be followed, nearly to the letter, or else anyone who is a Packer will soon be an ex-Packer.

The system boils down to this: You have been deemed, as a member of this team, to be smart enough, able enough, talented enough to go into a game at a moment's notice and perform. No excuses about being tired or not knowing the offense or bad communication will suffice.

If you're called on to play, go in and do the job because the system says you've been trained well enough to do it. If the starter goes down, his backup knows the drill.

Period. Any questions?

Perhaps at no time during the 1996 season did Holmgren's system come into play more critically than when the Packers hosted the pesky Detroit Lions on a glorious autumn afternoon.

The Packers were clearly sputtering on offense after losing two of their best wide receivers in Robert Brooks and Antonio Freeman.

But there was no time for wailing and making excuses. There were backups and they had to come in and perform. Beebe already had proven he could do the job with his scintillating performance three weeks earlier against San Francisco.

So who would step into the other wideout slot opposite Beebe?

The Packers had grown so desperate that they contacted the dismayed and disgruntled Anthony Morgan, who had started eight games the previous season and caught a career-high 31 passes, four for touchdowns.

However, Morgan had been outplayed in training camp by Freeman and on the final cutdown before the start of the season, Morgan was released in what general manager Ron Wolf called one of the toughest personnel moves he'd ever had to make.

Morgan, who had also been suffering from back problems, apparently had moved on with his life and was beginning a business in the Chicago area when the Packers called.

Knowing Green Bay was desperate and still smarting after being released, Morgan played hardball with the Packers, demanding the same salary he'd made when he was released.

Eventually, the two sides came to an agreement and Morgan was signed the week before

Fourth-year cornerback Doug Evans had a breakthrough season and, according to many, should have been in the Pro Bowl. "I needed to get my foot in the door this year," Evans said. "I did that." And he did it by posting 78 tackles, a career-best five interceptions and defensing a team-best 15 passes. Against the Lions, he had one of his better games with five tackles and a sack.

▶ For a while during midseason, coach Mike Holmgren had to wonder what else could go wrong after losing his two best wide receivers in Robert Brooks and Antonio Freeman. But he patched together enough of an offense to beat the Lions, 28-18.

▲ **Two key members of the offensive line: center Frank Winters (left) and right tackle Earl Dotson.**

The receiver with the most experience in Holmgren's complex offense was a kid who had seven career receptions and had not seen a snap all regular season due to an ankle injury.

Third-year pro Terry Mickens was battling with Freeman in training camp for the split end job when he suffered a serious high ankle sprain in a preseason game against Pittsburgh. Though deemed minor early, the sprain never got any better and Mickens lost valuable time. As a result, Freeman won the split end job.

Now, nine weeks into the season, Mickens was ready – or at least as close as he'd ever get.

You see, the system was calling. The Packers needed Mickens and Mickens had to respond.

So he did.

In his first game back, he caught a career-high seven passes for 52 yards and grabbed 2- and 6-yard touchdown throws from Favre.

It was the chance the soft-spoken receiver had always sought but never really been in a position to get.

"I never really dwelled on that," Mickens said. "I just kept my head up and contributed where I could. All around, we have good talent at receiver. It's good to know that if someone goes down, we have other people who can step in."

The system. See?

Beebe also came up with another big afternoon, catching four passes for 106 yards, including a touchdown. And that came aftertaking ferocious hits from Detroit defensive backs that left him sprawled and dazed on the turf.

Beebe's touchdown was scored with 1:08 left in the third quarter and for all practical purposes, put the game out of reach.

Green Bay led 21-10 when Favre faked a handoff to Edgar Bennett. Beebe used a great move down the right sideline to get away from cornerback Ryan McNeil. Favre found Beebe at midfield and he used his speed to run away from the Lions defenders for a 65-yard score.

From there, the Packers defense took over.

True, Lions' tailback Barry Sanders had a superb day, rushing for 152 yards on 20 carries. But after a halftime tongue-lashing from Holmgren, the Packer defenders perked up and shut down Detroit.

"I almost ripped up the things the defensive coaches were talking about," Holmgren said. "I

the Lions game. "It's great to be back," he said.

The Packers were pleased because they had a receiver who knew the offense better than anyone they had. Actually, though, that wasn't entirely accurate.

said, 'This is not going to do it, diagraming this and that.' It's about playing harder, playing with more emotion."

And no one on defense did that better than tackle Santana Dotson.

Acquired in the offseason as a free agent signee from Tampa Bay to help shore up a suspect interior defense, Dotson made his presence felt against the Lions. He was credited with only two tackles, but Dotson sacked Detroit quarterback Don Majkowski twice, hurried him four other times, knocked him down three times, forced a fumble and batted down two passes in one of the more dominating performances by a Packers lineman in a long time.

"I was (single covered) and, as talented as our defensive line is, somebody has to make a play," Dotson said. "I was able to get up the field and get some good pressure."

Once again, the Packers had managed to survive. Despite being crippled on offense, Favre still found enough out there to throw for 281 yards and four touchdowns.

"A couple of days ago, you guys (the media) were trying to figure out what we were going to do," Favre said. "Now you say it doesn't matter who's out there. Funny how a game changes things."

▲ Roderick Mullen proved to be one of those versatile players the Packers could plug in at cornerback or safety. He also played some in Green Bay's six-defensive backs scheme and was a special teams terror.

▲ One reason the Packers defense improved so dramatically was the play of second-year linebacker Brian Williams. His stellar play in training camp forced the Packers coaching staff to find a place for him on the field. As a result, Williams moved into George Koonce's old spot at right linebacker and Koonce moved to the middle. "We simply had to play him," coach Mike Holmgren said. "It jumped out at you."

Seeing Red

November 10: Chiefs 27, Packers 20

Brett Favre confers with quarterbacks coach Marty Mornhinweg during Green Bay's 27-20 loss to the Kansas City Chiefs. Mornhinweg assumed the role previously held by Steve Mariucci, who left the Packers after the 1995 season to become head coach at the University of California. But in the rapid-fire world of the NFL, little stays the same. In 1997, Mariucci will be the new head coach of the San Francisco 49ers and Mornhinweg will be his offensive coordinator.

THERE ARE GAMES IN EVERY SEASON WHEN IT'S JUST NOT THERE. You wonder why and you try to correct it. You scream, you complain, you whine, but nothing changes.

It is, as they say, just one of those days. And on a dank, dreary, depressing day at Kansas City's Arrowhead Stadium, the Packers found themselves hip-deep in one of those days.

Things that hadn't happened to the Packers all season rose up on this day and nothing they tried to stop it seemed to make a difference.

"Tough game," Holmgren conceded afterward. "We battled to the end but we were too sloppy today. We didn't deserve to win this one."

And though Green Bay lost by just seven points, there was never really a feeling all day that the Packers were in it or, even at the end, had a chance to win.

It was, well, one of those days.

What was especially shocking was the way the Chiefs shredded the Packers' proud run defense.

The tandem of Greg Hill and Marcus Allen did most of the damage, with Hill gaining 94 yards and scoring twice and Allen adding 48 yards on 10 carries. Overall, Kansas City rushed for 182 yards and savaged the Packers defense for 383 yards, the most Green Bay would give up all season.

"I didn't think anybody could run on us like that," defensive end Sean Jones said.

Safety LeRoy Butler just shook his head in amazement.

"They just came out and ran the ball on us," Butler said. "They said, 'Whatever you want to throw at us, we'll be ready for it.' You've got to give them a lot of credit."

Tackle Santana Dotson said it was a matter of keeping the Packers guessing all day.

"They started off with Marcus and came back with Greg Hill," Dotson said. "It was a nice combination and it kept us off balance.

It appeared obvious from the start that this wouldn't be Green Bay's afternoon. On the first play from scrimmage, Kansas City quarterback Steve Bono hooked up with wide receiver Sean LaChappelle on a 69-yard bomb that resulted in a field goal.

The Packers responded with one of their own to tie the game, but things shortly went downhill for the Packers after that.

Early in the second quarter, Bono aimed a pass for wide receiver Tamarick Vanover, on which cornerback Doug Evans appeared to have excellent coverage.

Back judge Tim Millis disagreed, flagging Evans for pass interference. Evans went ballistic, charging the official and putting his hands on him in disbelief. Evans was nailed for a 15-yard unsportsmanlike conduct penalty and was tossed from the game.

"I was shocked by the call and I just...it

With Green Bay's woes at wide receiver, Terry Mickens finally got a chance to shine. In training camp, he was in a battle with Antonio Freeman to take over the split end job, but an ankle injury sidelined Mickens until November 3 against Detroit. In that game, he caught a career-best seven passes, including two touchdowns. And in a four-week span while Green Bay was struggling with its offense, he caught 18 passes for 161 yards.

was a reaction where I just grabbed him in the back like, oh,..." Evans said. "It wasn't like a push on purpose or anything like that. I put my hands on him. I guess that's what they threw me out for."

The call stunned the Packers.

"Doug Evans is the last guy that should get thrown out of a game," Holmgren said. "He's the nicest guy I've got. But you can't touch the official."

For the next quarter and a half, the game spiraled out of Green Bay's control as Kansas City scored 17 unanswered points in the second quarter and led 20-6 at the half.

When Favre fumbled the opening snap of

the third quarter and the Chiefs recovered, Hill broke four tackles and scored from 24 yards out to bump KC's lead to 27-6.

"It got to the point where you're looking for something to sway the momentum," safety Eugene Robinson said. "An interception or something that's a momentum-turner. And when you're doing that, you're losing."

The defense finally pulled itself together and slowed the Chiefs down, but the Green Bay offense could not take advantage. Favre did throw a 25-yard scoring pass to Beebe in the third quarter but another promising drive was stopped when Brian Washington picked off a Favre pass.

▲ Rookie Derrick Mayes celebrates his first NFL touchdown. Unfortunately for the Packers, it was too little, too late.

▲ Jeff Thomason, cut by the Packers two seasons ago, rebounded to make the squad the last two years as Green Bay's No. 3 tight end. Though he caught but three passes, his expertise was on special teams, where he posted 11 tackles.

Green Bay closed to within seven with 1:02 to play when Favre hit rookie Derrick Mayes for a touchdown. But the Packers didn't come close to recovering Craig Hentrich's onside kick and that was that.

The Packers gained 360 total yards against the Chiefs' highly touted defense and Favre threw for 310. But it was perhaps the quietest 300-yard day in his career.

"There's no shock," Jones said. "If we'd played well and they'd found some way to beat us, then there might be some shock. But we didn't play well enough to win against a very good football team. But we're still 8-2."

▲ Coach Mike Holmgren argues with referee Bob McElwee after cornerback Doug Evans was ejected from the game for touching an official while arguing a pass interference call. The Packers defense never quite recovered from Evans' loss and fell to the Chiefs.

▶ Another special teams demon was linebacker Lamont Hollinquest. He also saw action as a backup to right linebacker Brian Wiliams and posted a season-opening interception.

The Lambeau Leap

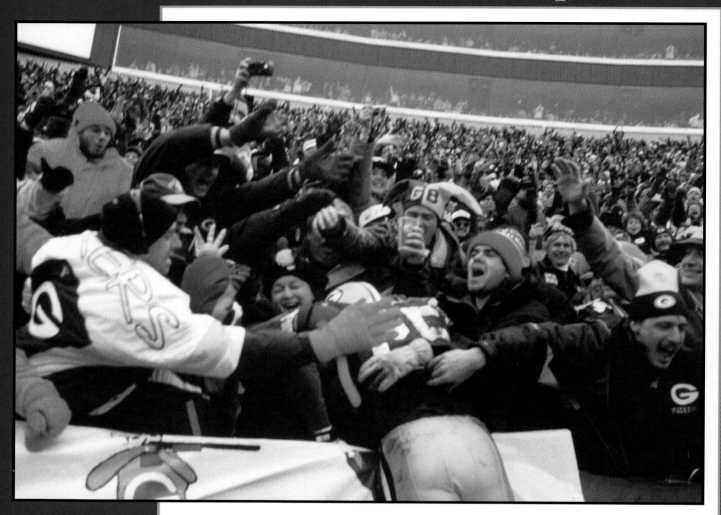

The origins go back just three seasons.

Yet it seems like the little piece of acrobatics now known as the "Lambeau Leap" have been around since the days of leather helmets.

Let LeRoy Butler, the originator, explain.

"It was 1993 and we were playing the Raiders in Lambeau Field," Butler said. "It was about 42 degrees below. The field was frozen. Everything was frozen. What happened was, they threw a screen, I hit the running back and Reggie White picked up the fumble and was running with it. One of the linemen grabbed him, he spun, caught my eye and pitched the ball to me.

"So I caught it and started running down the field. As I was running, the crowd was going crazy. They were reaching down and patting the side of the stadium. It was all spontaneous. I jumped up there and it was the greatest thing. It was so loud. The fans felt as if they were in the game and it seemed from then on that our fans looked forward to it. I think it's been great."

Still, The Leap didn't really catch on until 1995, when Robert Brooks took to taking half-gainers into the stands, and by midseason, nearly every Packer who scored took the plunge.

In '96, the tradition was refined and even improved (two jumpers at a time, for instance), but the Packers did stop jumping in the stands on the road after Brooks was clocked by a Vikings fan in Minneapolis.

Also, Brett Favre won't jump — his teammates claim he can't. Wide receiver Antonio Freeman stopped doing it to protect his broken arm and tight ends Keith Jackson and Mark Chmura won't try it, either.

But others can't wait.

When Andre Rison scored his first touchdown as a Packer, the first thing he did was dive into the sea of humanity.

"There was no way I wasn't going to do that," he said.

A sign of how The Leap has grown can be seen around the league as other players started jumping into the seats as well.

"I think it's great," coach Mike Holmgren said. "As long as they throw them back."

Brett Favre

To reach heaven, Brett Favre had to go through hell.

For the Green Bay quarterback, 1996 will be remembered as the best of times and the worst of times.

It will be remembered as the year that began with his coronation as the NFL's most valuable player.

It will be remembered as the year when he somberly stood in front of a packed press conference in May and admitted an addiction to prescription painkillers.

It will be remembered as the year his longtime girlfriend Deanna Tynes threatened to leave him if he didn't get help.

It will be remembered as the year when his best friend, Mark Haverty, was killed in a car accident in which Brett's brother, Scott, was driving.

It will be remembered as the year his sister, Brandi, was implicated in a drive-by shooting.

But it will also be remembered as the year Favre married Deanna after he got out of the drug rehab clinic.

It will be remembered as the year he proved all the critics wrong and had an even better season than 1995, this time with an NFC-record 39 touchdown passes.

It will be remembered as the year he matured and grew both as a quarterback and human being.

It will be remembered as the year he finally shook off the label of the best quarterback never to reach a Super Bowl as he directed Green Bay past New England.

"I don't think Brett ever wants to go through a year like he had last year," coach Mike Holmgren said.

Favre agreed.

And after throwing for 246 yards and two touchdowns and running for a third in Super Bowl XXXI, Favre has put his imprint once and for all on the Packers and on the NFL.

"This (the Super Bowl title) means everything," he said. "I've been through a lot of tough times and a lot of good times. They both kind of equal themselves out and you take the good with the bad. To win this, it's unbelievable. It definitely makes this past year a little better."

There's no doubt that Favre was under a microscope far more than he's been at any other time in his career. Or his life. And everyone was looking for the same thing — a sign of weakness, a hesitation, something that said Favre was cracking under the pressure.

Nobody ever saw it.

Once again, Favre started every game for the Packers, 19 this season and an improbable 87 straight overall, including the playoffs. And though he was thrown around this season like some Doberman's chew toy, Favre always came back. Always.

"He's just a tough guy," said tight end Mark Chmura, one of Favre's closest friends.

And though Favre had his off-season and off-field problems, the key was that he never changed.

"He's the same guy who likes to have fun in the locker room," said center Frank Winters, another of Brett's pals. "He's a lot of fun to be around. He's a jokester. The people who don't know him wonder how he is, but he's the same as he was before. He's just a good, old country boy."

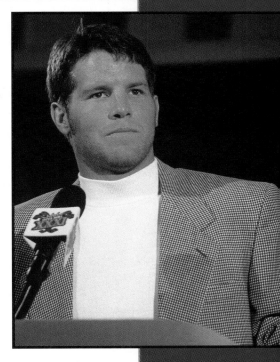

After another remarkable year, Holmgren expects this to be a whirlwind off-season for Favre. But he also expects the 27-year-old to act more responsibly than he did the previous off-season, when events conspired to overwhelm him.

"His off season, if possible, will be more hectic than last year," Holmgren said. "He's the two-time MVP of the league. He's the Super Bowl quarterback. He's on the verge of signing one of those unbelievable contracts (reportedly a seven-year, $50 million extension). He's engaging. He's funny. People want him for everything and he'll be tugged in a million different directions."

Holmgren, who serves as almost a surrogate parent, has advised Favre how to handle his increasing fame.

"It was the same conversation we've had for the last five years," Holmgren said. "You have to be discerning. You have to understand what you want. You don't have to do everything. It will be a great challenge to him. The lessons he learned last year, while painful, were valuable."

Favre even caused a brief stir late in the season when he mentioned to a Mississippi TV station that he really wasn't sure how much longer he wanted to play football.

When asked about it, Favre's response was telling.

"I just meant that I don't want to get to a certain age and not be able to play with my kids because I'm so beat up," he said. "I don't want someone telling me when it's time to go. I want to leave on my own terms."

That's the only way it could be with Brett Favre.

Same Old Story
November 18: Cowboys 21, Packers 6

HIS TIME IT WOULD BE DIFFERENT, THE GREEN BAY PACKERS SAID. Watch.

No, really, just wait and see.

If the Packers had done nothing else after absorbing six straight losses to the Dallas Cowboys at Texas Stadium, they had at least learned how to talk with the kind of bravado normally reserved for teams that have won world titles.

Unfortunately, their confident words the week before their latest battle with the hated Cowboys sounded more like whistling past a graveyard. In truth, the Packers, after losing six straight times in the prairie, still didn't have a clue how to stop the Cowboys.

Yes, they were certainly better than they were the first few trips down there when the Cowboys toyed with them like a cat paws a wounded canary.

In 1995, especially in the NFC title game, the Packers showed they had clearly made strides against Dallas, battling well into the fourth quarter before finally losing again.

Now, on the Packers' third and final Monday night appearance of the season, they had a chance to prove just how far they'd come. Beneath the bold words, however, was a deep-seated realization that they were going to war with a broom.

The Packers knew their defense was top

drawer, but the offense? Oh my.

Robert Brooks was gone for the year with a knee injury. Antonio Freeman was still three weeks away from coming back after breaking a bone in his arm. The casualty list also included Pro Bowl tight end Mark Chmura, who collapsed the week before in Kansas City after tearing the arch in his foot.

So three of Green Bay's key weapons were gone at exactly the time they were needed most.

In truth, the game that looked like one of the NFL's top matchups at the beginning of the season turned out to be something of a snooze.

The Cowboys were struggling on offense as well, so coupled with Green Bay's woes, it was not exactly the game football fans had hoped to see.

In fact, the star was a field goal kicker – Cowboy Chris Boniol, who tied an NFL record by kicking seven against the Packers.

"It's very painful any time you lose and obviously you come down here and play the world champions and really didn't play as well as you had anticipated," general manager Ron Wolf said. "It hurts."

There was a special sting because the Packers defense held the Cowboys to a mere 317 total yards, an effort that normally would have been good enough. But the offense just could not cope with the loss of

Unlike past meetings, the Packers did not let Cowboys' quarterback Troy Aikman destroy them. Here, Reggie White gets good pressure on Aikman. For the game, Aikman threw for just 205 yards and no touchdowns.

► A meeting of the minds at midfield prior to the Monday night game between Packers' coach Mike Holmgren and Dallas' Barry Switzer. The post-game meeting, after a last-second Cowboys' field goal, wouldn't be quite so cordial.

▲ Brett Favre once again struggled against the Cowboy's quick, athletic defense. He completed 21 of 37 passes for 194 yards and was sacked twice.

so many key players.

"Who'd have thought we could hold them without a touchdown and lose?" Favre said. "But I knew coming in it would be a tough game and that they have a tough defense."

Favre was harassed all night by the quick, mobile Cowboys front line and ended up completing just 21 of 37 passes for only 194 yards. Green Bay's only touchdown came with 1:53 to play when Favre hooked up with Mayes for a 3-yard score.

What followed was probably the highlight of the evening and may provide ample fuel for the Packers-Cowboys rivalry that seems to grow by the hour.

Leading 18-6 in the final minute, Dallas got

the ball on the Packers 37 after a failed onside kick. After a Sherman Williams 20-yard run, the Cowboys were in position to score again. And when Cowboys coach Barry Switzer learned Boniol needed one more field goal to tie a league record, he sent him out to drill a 28-yarder with 20 seconds to play.

The Packers, unaware of the record, were incensed by the kick, feeling that the Cowboys were unnecessarily piling it on.

"They just wanted to rub our faces in it," Butler said. "Like a little kid, nah, nah, nah...It was a joke. Even the referees were complaining, 'Aww, I can't believe this.' "

Reggie White and linebacker Wayne Simmons were particularly annoyed, walking over to the Cowboys bench and gesturing emphatically. White and Dallas wide receiver Michael Irvin even jawed at each other menacingly for a few seconds, though they talked cordially after the game.

"That's not important," White said afterward. "They did it. They won. They beat us. That's what it all boils down to. If we wouldn't have allowed them to be in that position, they wouldn't have done it."

For the Packers, it was their seventh straight defeat at the hands of the Cowboys, all in Dallas.

Though they clearly had made strides against the main nemesis, facts were facts: The Packers still could not beat the Cowboys. And until they did, they would never be considered among the NFL's elite.

Or so it seemed at the time.

◄ The Packers were operating at less than half strength on offense with the losses of wide receivers Antonio Freeman and Robert Brooks and Pro Bowl tight end Mark Chmura. Don Beebe, here being blanketed by Dallas cornerback Kevin Smith, tried to fill the void, but the Packers simply didn't have the weapons to compete. "It's a shame we couldn't have played them at full strength," Favre said.

▲ The only dent the Packers were able to make offensively came in the final minute when Brett Favre threw a touchdown pass to Derrick Mayes. It was Mayes' third catch in two games and two went for touchdowns.

Ramming Speed
November 24: Packers 24, Rams 9

ENOUGH WAS ENOUGH.

The Packers had played two of their poorer games of the season and had lost them both. They stood at 8-3 and their once-insurmountable lead in the NFC Central Division was suddenly in jeopardy.

The offense was still struggling, the defense hadn't forced a turnover in three games and the Packers, who had looked so formidable most of the season, appeared to be cracking.

If Green Bay was going to turn its season around, it had to start now. Against the struggling St. Louis Rams. In the new Trans World Dome by the banks of the Mississippi River.

The Packers hoped to get a boost from controversial wide receiver Andre Rison, who had been released the previous Monday by Jacksonville and scooped up a day later by Ron Wolf.

Green Bay had gone after Rison hard two years earlier, when he was a free agent after a stormy but successful career with the Atlanta Falcons. The Pack was looking for someone to replace the retired Sterling Sharpe because, at the time, no one was sure Robert Brooks was the guy who could do it.

Despite a long courtship, Rison spurned the Packers and signed with the Browns – a decision he regretted almost immediately.

Rison left the Browns after one season and signed with the Jaguars. But he never hit it off with head coach Tom Coughlin or quarterback Mark Brunell and he was released.

Knowing Rison's background, but also knowing the Packers could not survive much longer without a legitimate threat at wide receiver, Wolf and Holmgren took the chance, releasing Anthony Morgan yet again and claiming Rison off waivers.

Holmgren told Rison that as far he was concerned, the slate was clean and he had a new start in Green Bay. So make the best of it.

"From day one, when I came into this organization, it's the first time I've seen open arms," Rison said. "I've been welcomed. That made my job easier."

With that backdrop, the Packers prepared for the nationally televised Sunday night game against the team that had handed Green Bay its last home loss in September of 1995.

And the latest festivities did not start well.

Spurred by a raucous sellout crowd, the young Rams flew around on defense and made life miserable for Favre and the Packers.

On offense, the Rams didn't have a lot of weapons, but they were just dangerous enough to spring the upset.

Trouble escalated in the second quarter when the Rams finally put a drive together behind the throwing of rookie quarterback Tony Banks and the running of rookie tailback Lawrence Phillips.

St. Louis marched 69 yards in 13 plays

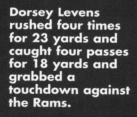

Dorsey Levens rushed four times for 23 yards and caught four passes for 18 yards and grabbed a touchdown against the Rams.

▶ **In what may have turned out to be the key play of the Packers' season, cornerback Doug Evans returned an interception 32 yards for a touchdown to open the third quarter, and put the Packers on top to stay, 10-9.**

▲ **Defensive end Gabe Wilkins introduces himself to fallen St. Louis quarterback Tony Banks.**

and scored when Banks hit wide receiver Isaac Bruce in the back of the end zone.

It got worse for the Packers.

Forced to start the next drive at his own 5-yard line, Favre was pressured by Rams end Kevin Carter and while back in the end zone, he flung a pass underhanded to absolutely no one in particular in an effort to avoid a sack.

The officials weren't buying it and Favre was flagged for intentional grounding in the end zone, which resulted in a safety and a 9-0 Rams lead.

Now the Packers were in trouble. The crowd was into the game and the Packers were doing nothing on offense. Somebody, somewhere had to step in and stop the bleeding.

That someone was veteran backup safety Mike Prior, who made what may have been one of the biggest plays of the Packers season.

On the ensuing free kick from punter Craig Hentrich following the safety, the ball bounced behind a line of St. Louis blockers and in front of the return men. Like a kickoff, this was a

free ball. Prior, streaking down the left sideline, leaped on the ball and held on despite being clobbered so hard by several Rams his helmet flew off.

No matter, the Packers had the ball at the St. Louis 37 with two minutes left in the first half. And though Prior's recovery only resulted in a field goal for Green Bay, it was huge because it slowed St. Louis' momentum, took the crowd out of the game and gave the Packers at least a glimmer of hope heading into the locker room.

"That really got us going," defensive tackle Santana Dotson said. "It got the whole team fired up."

And everyone showed it at the start of the third quarter.

On St. Louis' second offensive play, Banks tried to thread a pass to wide receiver Johnny Thomas, but cornerback Doug Evans cut underneath the pattern, picked it off and scooted 32 yards for a touchdown – and a sudden 10-9 lead.

"We wanted to make the ball the issue after going three games without a turnover," Evans said. "Turnovers are the key to success for us. Turnovers win ballgames. The ball was the key issue."

The Packers went on to force two more turnovers and Favre threw touchdown passes to Keith Jackson and Dorsey Levens and Green Bay, despite gaining just 226 yards, pulled out a game it had to have.

"We get Antonio Freeman back next week, which will help us," Holmgren said. "So I'm hoping now we can get it rolling again and peak at the right time."

As for Rison, he caught a team-high five passes for 44 yards – including a couple of acrobatic jobs. Not only that, but the reborn wideout clearly brought electricity to the Packer bench and he hugged Favre so many times on the sideline that it appeared they'd been friends for life.

The Packers?

No one was positive, not yet, but it seemed they had weathered the storm.

▲ Santana Dotson congratulates safety LeRoy Butler for recovering a Tony Banks fumble. The Green Bay defense held the Rams to 84 total yards in the second half and forced three turnovers.

◄ Don Beebe heads out of bounds after catching a pass. In the six-game period when the Packers were without their complement of receivers, Beebe stepped up to catch 26 balls for 457 yards and three touchdowns.

Chapter 5
Back On The Offensive
December 1: Packers 28, Bears 17

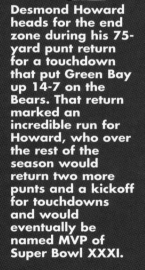

FOR THE BETTER PART OF A MONTH, THE PACKERS WERE AWOL, Acutely Without Offensive Leverage.

A series of debilitating injuries, first to No. 1 receiver Robert Brooks (a season-ending knee injury), then to No. 2 wideout Antonio Freeman (a broken bone in his arm) and then to Pro Bowl tight end Mark Chmura (torn foot arch), had left the Packers reeling on offense.

Since the injury bug had bitten, the Packers had gone 4-2 but scared no one while doing it. The offense, the most prolific in the game, was averaging just 19 points a game over that span. And while the offense was also churning out a respectable 326 total yards during the same period, in the last two games, the Packers had managed just 254 yards against the Dallas Cowboys and an even more anemic 243 against St. Louis.

This was not what Green Bay needed heading into the stretch run.

Fortunately for coach Mike Holmgren, there was a light at the end of the tunnel in the person of Freeman, the talented wide receiver who had missed most of five games after breaking his ulnar bone against Tampa Bay on Oct. 27.

In a perfect world, Freeman probably would have sat out another game or two to make sure the bone was healing properly. But the Packers had no more time to spare.

The offense was struggling and the defense couldn't keep it's finger in the dike all season.

So Freeman, who had been running and staying in shape almost since he hurt himself, was given the OK to play in a critical NFC Central Division battle with the Bears.

And it was a memorable return indeed.

Wearing a bulky, padded cast to protect the tender arm, Freeman abused the Bears all afternoon, catching 10 passes for 156 yards, both career-bests, as the offense sprang back to life.

"It's just a pleasure to be back," said a beaming Freeman after the game.

But it was an ominous start at best for the receiver, who had trouble hanging onto the ball all of 1995 as a rookie. On Green Bay's fourth play from scrimmage, Brett Favre connected with Freeman for four yards but as he was hit from behind, Freeman fumbled, though he gathered in the loose ball himself.

"When you come back from an injury, you always need that first hit to get you going," he said. "That was the first hit and I knew what I had to do after that."

What he did, on the next series, was make a nice sideline move and gather in a 41-yard bomb from Favre, the longest pass play to a wide receiver in a month.

"I was very excited to have him back," Favre said. "I was kind of surprised he was able to come in and catch the ball as well as he did in such a short time."

So Freeman was back and Favre meant to take full advantage of it. In fact, though the

Desmond Howard heads for the end zone during his 75-yard punt return for a touchdown that put Green Bay up 14-7 on the Bears. That return marked an incredible run for Howard, who over the rest of the season would return two more punts and a kickoff for touchdowns and would eventually be named MVP of Super Bowl XXXI.

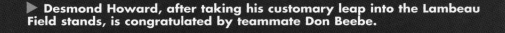

▶ **Desmond Howard, after taking his customary leap into the Lambeau Field stands, is congratulated by teammate Don Beebe.**

▲ Tight end Keith Jackson beats Chicago's rookie cornerback Walt Harris to the corner of the end zone for a touchdown that tied the game at 7-7. At that stage, Jackson had 34 receptions on the season, eight for touchdowns.

▶ Wide receiver Antonio Freeman, sidelined nearly five full games with a broken ulnar bone in his left arm, returned wearing a specially padded cast. The results were stunning as Freeman caught 10 passes for 156 yards, both career highs. "I may never take that cast off again," Freeman said.

Packers had the ball for just 18 offensive plays in the first half, Favre threw to Freeman seven times, completing five for 101 yards.

Freeman helped set up Green Bay's only score of the half with catches of 15 and 30 yards and in the second half, he caught five more passes, three of which went for first downs.

"It was good to have him back," coach Mike Holmgren said. "I talked to him before the game about really concentrating, because I knew he was excited and he has this thing on his arm. And I reminded him that he did drop a few passes (before he was hurt). But I think he had a great game."

As for the cast?

"It's my lucky charm," Freeman said. "I may never take it off again."

Freeman wasn't the only welcome addition to the offense. Fullback Dorsey Levens, relegated to a backup role behind William Henderson for much of the season, burst onto the scene as well, spelling halfback Edgar Bennett and giving a badly needed boost to the running game.

Against Chicago, Levens was used as Green Bay's single back in three- or four-wideout sets and he flourished in the role, rushing for a career-high 69 yards on just five carries and scoring a touchdown. And all of it came in the second half.

"He's a good runner and good football player," Holmgren said. "Given the chance, he'll get his yards."

But that also has been the problem for the third-year back from Georgia Tech. Levens was caught in a bind between the veteran halfback in Bennett and the hulking Henderson, a better blocker.

Against the Bears, though, Levens proved to be an excellent alternative, keeping Chicago off balance all day.

"There were some gaping holes," Levens said. "All you've got to do is make some people miss and you're in the secondary."

It was also Levens' 10-yard burst off right tackle with 12:40 remaining in the fourth quarter that staked the Packers to a 21-10 lead and gave them the cushion they needed.

Levens' performance helped the Green Bay running game pile up 126 yards, the most it had gained on the ground since it racked up

Dorsey Levens bursts through the Bears line on his way to another big gain. For the first time during the season, coach Mike Holmgren decided to use Levens more as a running back to spell Edgar Bennett. The plan immediately paid dividends as Levens shredded the Bears for 69 yards on just five carries.

129 yards against the Buccaneers Oct. 27.

And there was still more.

The running and the passing game clicked, but so did the special teams, thanks to Desmond Howard's 75-yard punt return for a touchdown.

Howard's return, his second for a touchdown this season, broke a 7-7 tie in the third quarter and sent the Bears, who have come to expect imminent disaster when facing the Packers, spinning into despair.

"That just broke their backs," said Tyrone Williams, who delivered a key block to help spring Howard loose. "You saw it. The air went right out of them. We started running the ball down their throats. That just turned the whole game around."

Howard, who normally needs just the smallest of cracks to get free, didn't have to worry about that.

"Usually you have to make a couple of moves to go untouched," he said. "I didn't have to make many."

In fact, Howard wasn't touched the entire time and when he made punter Todd Sauerbrun slip at midfield, he knew he was gone.

"We lost containment, I guess," Bears coach Dave Wannstedt said. "Or we got blocked. It was just poor coverage."

The Packers got exactly what they needed

from the game – a rejuvenated offense that picked up 342 yards, a defense that allowed just 292 yards and a special teams score.

"We're getting back to where we need to be," Favre said. "And it's about time."

Andre Rison, picked up off waivers Nov. 19 by the desperate Packers, wasted little time fitting in. He caught five passes in his first game as a Packer in St. Louis then added two catches against the Bears. But while his numbers weren't spectacular, he forced defenses to account for him, thus opening up more opportunities for other weapons.

Reggie White

What is the enduring image of Reggie White?

Is it his three sacks in Super Bowl XXXI, when he simply decided his time had come and so he made Patriots right tackle Max Lane look like a speed bump?

Is it his emotional appeals during pregame warmups, as he points and waves and gestures to a raucous Lambeau Field crowd? Or maybe it was when he skipped around the frozen field after the NFC title game, again saluting the fans?

Or perhaps it was after the Super Bowl, when he sprinted around the Superdome, the Lombardi Trophy held high?

Maybe it's none of the above. Or all the above.

Yet ask Reggie White and he'll tell you what he hopes people will remember about him after the Super Bowl.

"What if I did get a ring but never impacted anyone's life?" he said. "The ring don't mean a thing. I would like to get the ring and continue to impact other people's lives."

And there is only one way to do that, as White sees it.

"God has given me the opportunity to do the things that I do because of professional football and given me the opportunity to lead people toward Christ," he said.

White doesn't apologize for his message, which he made clear as soon as the Packers reached the Super Bowl.

It is well-known that White, an ordained minister, may be the single biggest reason why religion has become such a big part of pro football.

Post-game prayer circles can be found at almost every game now. And White helped start it.

"We're just thanking God that we weren't killed in the game," he said.

But White has run into his share of doubters.

Four years ago, when he shocked pro football and sent free-agency spinning into a new direction by signing with the Packers, White said God told him where to go. Cynics claim it was the $17 million that directed him.

In 1995, he tore a hamstring that should've ended his season but returned two weeks later claiming God had healed him, many said he simply wasn't hurt that badly in the first place.

White has heard it all over the years. But instead of getting furious, he simply and quietly restates his position. If people agree, fine. If they don't, that's fine too.

"I just accept my role," he said. "I think in all of us is imbedded leadership qualities and if you want to be a follower, that's all you'll ever be. I accept my role as a leader, not only on this team, but in the community."

Now that White is a Super Bowl champion, he thinks his message will have an even larger audience.

"My championship lies in other peoples' lives being changed," he said. "I want to see people saved. I want to see the drug dealers' lives changed, the prostitutes' lives changed. I want to see people who are having a hard time and are oppressed and are poor, their lives changed for the benefit of the kingdom of God. That's the most important thing to me. How many people saw this game? Eight hundred million people around the world and 72,000 in the stadium. A lot of people saw us and I hope I was able in some kind of way to have an impact."

Fritz Shurmur And Sherm Lewis

Mike Holmgren may have been the brain, but Sherm Lewis and Fritz Shurmur were the soul.

They operated in the shadows, for the most part, content to do their jobs quietly but oh, so efficiently.

There was Lewis, Holmgren's longtime friend who was the offensive coordinator for the highest-scoring unit in football. And there was Shurmur, the 64-year-old wizard who constructed the best defense in the league.

Nice combination, eh?

Shurmur has been down the pike more than a few times. He has coached in the NFL since 1975, when he broke in with the Detroit Lions. Since then, he has been defensive coordinator for the New England Patriots, Los Angeles Rams, Arizona Cardinals and since 1994, the Packers.

The Green Bay defense has improved every year since Shurmur's arrival. But in 1996, he molded a unit that was truly something.

The Packers allowed a league-low 210 points and only 19 touchdowns, setting a record for a 16-game schedule.

Want more numbers? The defense allowed quarterbacks a rating of 55.4, the third-lowest of any NFL team in the 1990s and the lowest mark by a Packers opponent since 1974. Also, nearly 30 percent of every opponent's drives ended in three downs and a punt. And only in two games this season did the opposition score three straight times against the defense.

Overall, the defense allowed an average of 260 yards per game (88 rushing, and 171 passing) in the regular season. And this team which managed just 16 takeaways the season before forced 39 this time around.

More important, the defense was just as good in the playoffs, allowing an average of 234 yards and a total of 48 points in three games.

But do not call Shurmur a genius.

"This is football," he scoffed. "It's a game. I'm no genius. The real geniuses out there are the people who can feed a family of four on $20,000 a year. They're the geniuses."

Still, Shurmur has had his share of brainstorms, especially when it comes to slowing down high-powered offenses.

Since joining the Packers, in fact, Shurmur has devised defenses to beat the San Francisco 49ers three times. And in the Super Bowl, Shurmur heard all the talk about the nearly unstoppable Patriot offense. He wasn't exactly cocky, but...

After a rocky first quarter in which the Pats picked up 131 yards, Green Bay rallied and allowed just 126 yards the rest of the game.

"I don't know where he comes up with some of those schemes," marveled linebacker Ron Cox. "Maybe he sits out in his (ice-fishing) shed and draws them in the ice, I don't know. But they sure work."

If Shurmur is the reluctant genius, Lewis is the forgotten one.

Much of the credit for the Packers formidable offense has gone to Holmgren. But Lewis always has been lurking in the shadows, serving as Holmgren's sounding board, aide-de-camp and critic.

True, Holmgren calls nearly all the plays, but during the St. Louis game, when nothing was working, Holmgren handed the reins to Lewis and the Packers offense woke up.

Lewis, who worked with Holmgren in San Francisco, is affable and helpful, but won't go out of his way to seek the limelight.

"I think an assistant coach's role is to stay in the background," he said. "That's just the way I've been brought up. He's not supposed to be the most quotable guy. That's the head man's role and I've seen guys get themselves into trouble by always being the guy that had all the quotes. That's not my role."

Lewis' role was tough enough this season, as he had to juggle offensive personnel in the face of injuries. The result was a Packers offense that led the league with 456 points while churning out an average of 346 yards per game.

In fact, perhaps no one appreciates more how well this so-called "West Coast Offense" can run than Lewis.

"The way you go down and just cut a defense up," he said, "you just slice it. It's a beautiful thing."

And though Lewis maintains he's happy in his role, his ultimate goal is still to become a head coach. He interviewed last year at his alma mater, Michigan State, losing out to ex-NFL assistant Nick Saban. He also interviewed for the University of Kentucky job, too, but was not called.

Then, with a record 10 NFL openings this year, Lewis figured he'd at least get an interview, though rules forbid teams to talk to coaches whose teams are still in the playoffs.

Nonetheless, no one waited to talk to one of the brightest offensive minds in the NFL and two teams, St. Louis and New Orleans, even reached back into the archives to resurrect a couple of old-timers — Dick Vermeil and Mike Ditka — who had been out the game for years.

The lack of interest amazes Holmgren.

"(Lewis) has everything you need to be a head coach in this league," Holmgren said. "Someone is really missing the boat with Sherm."

Lewis shrugs it off.

"I'd like to be head coach, but I don't get consumed by it," he said. "I like working with Mike. I've got a good job here, I really do."

A Lambeau Field High

THIS WAS SUPPOSED TO BE A CLASSIC.

Brett Favre against John Elway. The AFC's best against one of the NFC's best. A great Denver offense against a great Green Bay defense. It had it all.

Well, almost.

Sometimes, and the Packers will be the first to admit it, it's better to be lucky than good. And it's best of all to be both.

The Packers, despite a nasty spate of injuries, had been pretty fortunate all season. They had faced the 49ers without Steve Young, their best quarterback. They met the Bears without their top quarterback, Erik Kramer. They beat Detroit without having to face quarterback Scott Mitchell. And they whipped the Rams without their hotshot rookie receiver Eddie Kennison.

Now the formidable Broncos came to town having wrapped up the AFC West title and home-field advantage throughout the playoffs just a week earlier.

Coach Mike Shanahan faced the question of whether to keep all his key players in the lineup to maintain continuity (also risking serious injury) or rest his stars and hope his team stayed on a roll.

It is never an easy question and Shanahan wrestled with it all week, especially regarding Elway, a serious MVP candidate who had pulled a hamstring muscle the week before and wasn't 100 percent.

The Packers practiced all week as though Elway would play, but it became clear as the week progressed that backup Bill Musgrave would get the nod.

As little as the game meant to the Broncos, it meant everything to the Packers, who were battling to gain precious home-field advantage themselves, and knew a win over Denver was another step in that direction.

"Whatever situation (Denver) was in, it couldn't affect how we played," coach Mike Holmgren said. "So we talked about that, setting a standard of play and playing up to that standard."

Besides, Holmgren knew a little about Musgrave after having coached him when both were with the 49ers. Holmgren knew that even though Musgrave didn't have much game experience, he was smart, resourceful and dangerous.

And as safety LeRoy Butler pointed out, the Packers haven't exactly dominated back-up quarterbacks in the past.

"Remember Jason Garrett?" he said, referring to the Dallas Cowboys' third-string quarterback who threw for more than 300 yards in a Thanksgiving Day win over the Packers in 1994.

Fortunately, all these concerns were misplaced.

The Packers, who had pulled themselves together the week before on offense, seemed back on their mission of gaining home-field advantage, squashing anyone who came in and then going to the Super Bowl and winning that.

The Broncos just happened to get in the way.

Favre threw for 280 yards and four touchdowns, Antonio Freeman continued

Antonio Freeman had good reason to smile. A week removed from a 10-catch, 156-yard effort against Chicago, he came back with nine catches for 175 yards and three touchdowns against the AFC powerhouse Denver Broncos.

his amazing comeback with nine catches for 175 yards and the defense completely shut down Denver, holding the Broncos to a mere 179 yards.

"Everybody was sharp, everybody knew what we needed to do or wanted to do to win this game," Broncos safety Tyrone Braxton said. "We just didn't go out and perform like we usually do."

Of course, the Packers might have had something to do with that.

And while it was true that Elway and All-Pro left tackle Gary Zimmerman didn't play, most of the rest of Denver's starting cast was front and center – including outstanding tailback Terrell Davis and tight end Shannon Sharpe.

But neither could do a thing. Davis rushed for just 54 yards on 14 carries and Sharpe caught four passes for only 34 yards – all of that in the first half.

"People may say, 'Well, Elway didn't play,' " defensive end Sean Jones said. "Well, Elway doesn't run the ball and we still did a pretty good job taking away the run."

Butler was superb, shutting down Sharpe in the frequent one-on-one matchups they had during the game. Butler also sacked Musgrave once and finished with six tackles.

"Shannon's like the best player on the whole offense, besides Elway," Butler said. "To know you did a pretty good job on him makes you feel good. It was a challenge for me to step up. I thought this was my biggest challenge."

While this game proved ultimately to be a rout, it was tight for a while as the two teams traded field goals early.

With Green Bay leading 6-3 in the final minute of the first half, Favre took the Packers 73 yards in seven plays and needed only 34 seconds to do it.

Working the two-minute offense to perfection, Favre hit Freeman for 17 yards to the Packers 44 on first down.

"The whole key in the two-minute offense is what happens on that first-down play," Holmgren said. "That pass was big. Now you can work. That first down is the key play and that allowed us to do some things."

Favre then followed with a pass to tight end Mark Chmura, who broke Braxton's tackle and

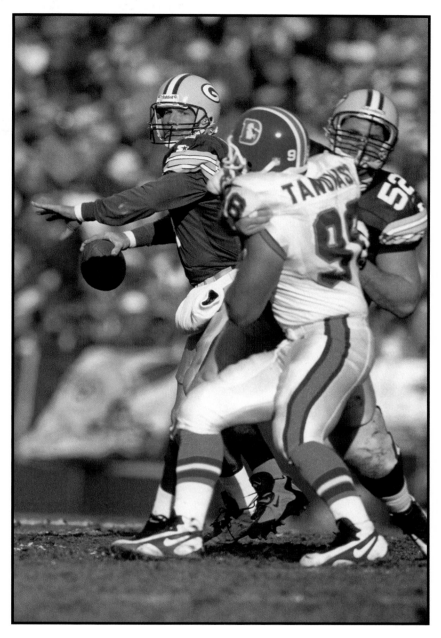

rumbled 29 yards to the Denver 27.

A Levens screen pass then netted eight yards and an Edgar Bennett run picked up five, putting the Packers on the Bronco 14.

Favre then dropped back, saw tackle Michael Dean Perry roaring toward him, straight-armed him to the ground, slipped to his right and hit Freeman in the back of the end zone for a touchdown with 17 seconds left.

"We needed some sort of lift," Favre said. "That was the momentum we needed to take into the second half."

Incredibly, the late drive marked the eighth time during the season (and the third straight game) the Packers scored points in the waning

▲ With all his weapons back again, Brett Favre threw for 280 yards and four touchdowns in his best performance in a month.

▲ Tight end Mark Chmura, out since Nov. 10 in Kansas City when he tore a foot arch, returned against the Broncos and not only caught four passes for a season-high 70 yards, but blocked superbly to help reignite the Packers running game.

▲ Antonio Freeman breaks away from Tory James' tackle and runs 51 yards for the touchdown, his second of the game.

moments of the first half.

The Packers also scored touchdowns just before halftime in the season-opener at Tampa Bay, the following week against Philadelphia and twice against the Bears in Chicago. Green Bay also had late field goals at home against Tampa Bay, in Kansas City and St. Louis and had scored a late touchdown the previous week against Chicago.

"We've always been very good in two-

minute," Favre said. "I think our guys are conscious of it. It's something we work on and execute very well."

In this case, the late touchdown turned a 6-3 game into a 13-3 contest and from there on it was all Green Bay.

After a Jason Elam field goal in the third quarter brought Denver within seven, the Packers responded with three straight Favre touchdown passes – two to Freeman and one

▲ Denver quarterback Bill Musgrave, subbing for the injured John Elway, has nowhere to hide as cornerback Doug Evans roars in on a blitz.

to tight end Keith Jackson.

The final humiliation for Denver came late when Green Bay backup tailback Travis Jervey fumbled into the end zone and Don Beebe fell on it for the touchdown.

"This is a great win for us," Jackson said. "We needed it, no matter who showed up. For us, it means everything."

▲ Coach Mike Holmgren commends defensive end Sean Jones on a great game in which he forced and recovered a fumble.

Lion In Wait

HE PACKERS WERE BACK ON TRACK.

The injuries were behind them and the motivation of gaining home-field advantage, and forcing teams to come to the winter wonderland called Lambeau Field, was proving a powerful impetus.

But if there was a concern, for Mike Holmgren it was his team's inability to get off to fast starts.

It had been a problem all season and Holmgren really didn't know why.

In fact, it was a direct opposite from 1995, when the Packers had come out of the blocks on fire, scoring on their opening drive nine times.

This season, they'd scored only three times the first time they'd touched the ball. Worse, their opening halves in many games had been simply horrible. Holmgren realized they could not afford to play badly in the first halves of playoff games if they hoped to stick around any length of time.

Knowing all of this, as well as the fact that a win would secure a first-round playoff bye, the Packers went into one of their least favorite haunts, the Pontiac Silverdome, to play the under-achieving but always dangerous Lions.

As has been the case all season, the Packers once again futzed around in the opening half, then woke up after intermission and slapped around a Detroit team that had long since given up on itself and its long-suffering coach, Wayne Fontes.

"I think one thing we haven't been get-

Brett Favre gives guard Adam Timmerman a pat after throwing a key block that helped Favre score on a quarterback sneak against Detroit.

ting credit for, we've had the toughest sched-ule in the league and look where we are right now," defensive end Reggie White said. "Now, the important thing is to just keep this thing going."

That was done, thanks again to an elec-trifying Desmond Howard punt return, a great performance by White and enough offense to put the Lions away.

But it wasn't easy.

In the first half, a Green Bay touchdown was called back because of a penalty, Brett Favre threw an interception in the end zone, another drive stalled at the 1-yard line – and there was an entertaining little sequence during which the Green Bay offense was penalized three straight times.

Then there was wide receiver Don Beebe's boo-boo.

With Green Bay leading 10-0 and dri-ving in the final seconds of the first half (yes, again...), Favre hit Beebe near the side-line at the Lions' 13. But Beebe thought the Packers still had a timeout left and instead of stepping out of bounds to set up at least a field goal, he spun in to try and make more yardage.

The clock ran out and Green Bay got nothing for its trouble.

"It was a stupid play," said the veteran Beebe. "It was probably the dumbest play I've made in my career, including high school. I thought we had a timeout left and

I was trying to make a play. What can I say? It was a dumb play."

When asked about it after the game, Holmgren was still seething.

"You'll have to ask him what he was thinking," he said. "I refuse to talk to him at this particular point."

Those were exactly the plays Holmgren was concerned about heading into the playoffs, the plays that spell the difference between going to the Super Bowl and going home.

But as they had all season, the Packers pulled themselves together, made some necessary halftime adjustments and crushed Detroit.

"This is where we need to be now," tight end Mark Chmura said.

And the Packers got there thanks in large measure to Howard, who admitted he, too, was on a mission after learning that week he'd been snubbed in Pro Bowl voting. Despite having run two punts back for touchdowns, he had been left off the Pro Bowl roster in favor of Carolina kickoff return man Michael Bates.

Even though Howard denied all week that the Pro Bowl business bothered him, he conceded after the Lions game that he'd been stung.

"Everyone in Green Bay figured I'd make the Pro Bowl," he said. "We were kind of perturbed and upset about that. I was upset about it for a while."

So naturally Howard took out his frustration on the Lions. He returned his first punt 22 yards to the Lions' 35, setting up a Chris Jacke field goal.

But it was Howard's second return that turned the tide. He took punter Mark Royals' kick at his own 8-yard line, started up the right side, cut left toward the middle of the field and got a great block from Calvin Jones. From there, Howard accelerated, eluded a half-hearted attempt by Royals at the 50 and was gone, giving Green Bay a 10-0 lead.

"There were a lot of key blocks out there and I just worked off those guys," Howard said. "Those guys work their butts off and I have a lot of appreciation for them. I made cuts here and there but I also made cuts off their blocks."

After he reached the end zone, Howard struck his Heisman Trophy pose, the same one

he did in 1991 after he scored a touchdown for Michigan against Notre Dame.

"It was something I just thought of at the moment," Howard said. "It's something I'd only have done in Michigan. I have a lot of special feelings about the state."

Howard totaled 167 yards on five punt returns, giving him 791 and setting an NFL record for most punt return yards in a season. The old mark was 692 yards by Miami's Fulton Walker in 1985.

"I figured I'd never smile again until I broke the record," Howard said, smiling. "Now I can smile again."

"Desmond jump-started us again," Holmgren said. "He gives you great confidence when he's back there because he catches the ball so easily. He's a great asset to our team."

▲ Trying to block, and actually blocking, Gilbert Brown, Green Bay's 325-pound nose tackle, proved to be two different problems altogether.

▲ Desmond Howard does it again. Stung by not making the Pro Bowl, Howard merely took a punt back 92 yards for a touchdown against the Lions and set the NFL record for most punt return yards in a season.

▲ Sean Jones sets his sights on another ball carrier — his two-year-old son, Dylan.

Oh, by the way, Howard wasn't done tormenting the Lions.

On their next possession, the Lions failed to move and again punted to the Packers. This time, Royals tried to punt away from Howard, who still grabbed the ball near the left sideline on the Packers 39, slipped through the first wave of tacklers and appeared on his way for another touchdown.

Howard finally got caught in traffic and Royals dragged him down 37 yards later at the Detroit 34.

While he admitted wishing he was going to the Pro Bowl, Howard put everything into perspective.

"They can't vote you into the playoffs," he said.

Meanwhile, Reggie White looked at the calendar and realized he'd better kick his game up a notch.

It had not been a typical Reggie year as age, injury and constant double-teams had produced his worst season statistically.

Also, White was in the final year of his con-

tract and extension talks hadn't produced anything concrete prior to the season. As a result, White broke off talks until the end of the year. And while he said it was because he could concentrate on football, many Packer fans assumed White was unhappy and would leave Green Bay.

All that talk stopped the Wednesday prior to the Detroit game, though, as White signed a five-year, $19 million extension that would allow him to finish out his career as a Packer. Moreover, he announced he'd be moving to Wisconsin when he retired and wanted to go into the Hall of Fame as a Packer.

White responded to the week's hoopla with perhaps his best game of the season, as he sacked quarterback Scott Mitchell twice and forced a fumble. It was only the second time all season White had two sacks in a game, the first coming Sept. 15 against San Diego.

While Holmgren thought the contract situation was weighing on Reggie's mind, White denied it.

"I don't think it was that," he said. "I just think it was a situation where I just knew, now's the time to step up. All of us did a good job of getting pressure on Mitchell. That's what we have to do."

White turned it up as well because he decided he couldn't let safety LeRoy Butler lead the team in sacks, which he'd done until White overtook him against Detroit.

"I just hope we'll be able to do it next week so LeRoy can't catch up," White joked.

The Packer offense continued to reshape itself, picking up 336 yards, 111 on the ground.

So the job was nearly complete. The Packers had wrapped up a first-round playoff bye and would play their first postseason game at home. A win the following Sunday over the Minnesota Vikings would wrap up home field through the playoffs.

It was there for the taking.

▲ The Packers past and present met when Brett Favre and Lions' backup quarterback Don Majkowski chatted after the game. Majkowski was Green Bay's starter in 1992 when he injured an ankle in the third game of the season. That's when Mike Holmgren turned to the raw Favre, who led the Packers to the win. He hasn't left the lineup since.

▲ An exuberant Mike Holmgren talks to his team after the 31-3 pounding of Detroit, a win that sewed up a first-round playoff bye and went a long way toward securing home-field advantage.

The Packers may not have had safety in numbers, but they sure had numbers from the safeties.

If there was a better tandem of safeties in the NFL than veterans LeRoy Butler and Eugene Robinson, the Packers will eat your chinstrap.

Between them, Robinson and Butler brought 19 years of experience to the party and they used all of it to help make the Packers the toughest team in the league to throw against.

"They're smart, veteran guys who just don't make a lot of mistakes," said Bob Valesente, Green Bay's secondary coach.

And they were virtually everywhere.

Butler and Robinson finished as

the team's second-and fourth-leading tacklers and combined to defense 26 passes. Butler added five interceptions and 6 1/2 sacks, earned a Pro Bowl berth and some serious consideration for NFL player of the year. Robinson, the league's leading active interceptor with 48, picked off a team-high six balls in the regular season and added two more in the playoffs.

"A great combination," Valesente said.

Winning a Super Bowl clearly was important to both players, but for different reasons.

Butler is one of the Packers' graybeards, the player with the second-highest seniority (seven years) in Green Bay behind placekicker Chris Jacke's eight seasons.

A second-round draft pick in 1990 under Lindy Infante, Butler remembers the bad old days when the Packers were going nowhere in a hurry.

"When I first got here, everything about the organization seemed old," Butler said. "When Mike (Holmgren) and Ron (Wolf) got here, everything seemed more new wave, more up to date. The things we're doing now are so different from when I first came here. Now, we're expected to win 11, 12, maybe 13 games a season."

It has not been an easy journey for Butler, who grew up in Jacksonville with malformed foot bones that forced him to wear corrective, bulky shoes for three years.

Then as a safety at Florida State, Butler played in the shadow of Deion Sanders.

Butler came to Green Bay, where his first two seasons were dismal at best as the Packers won just 10 games. But he got a new life under Holmgren and in 1993, Butler earned his first Pro Bowl berth and appeared to be one of the league's rising young stars.

But injuries and illness held him back the next two years and in the last pre-season, Wolf took a verbal jab at Butler by saying he needed to work out more in the off season.

"That didn't bother me," Butler said. "It just made me want to prove what I could do."

Which, quite likely, is what Wolf had in mind.

As a result, Butler had a superb 1996 season that started with two interceptions in the opener against Tampa Bay.

"The biggest thing he's underrated for is how smart he is," Robinson said. "That's a smart man. He knows what (offensive) guys are going to do almost before they do it."

In truth, Butler's superb season had a lot to do with the acquisition of Robinson, who was traded from Seattle to Green Bay for defensive end Matt LaBounty due to salary cap problems.

And yes, there were also questions about how much Robinson had left, especially after recovering from an Achilles tendon injury two years earlier.

But Robinson showed his savvy almost immediately both on the field and off, tutoring the young defensive backs about the importance of turnovers and making them stay after practice during training camp — and catching dozens of balls.

The results?

After 13 regular-season interceptions in 1995, the Packers came up with 26.

Robinson also helped Butler become a better player.

"Before, the coaches weren't comfortable with me taking chances because we didn't have a guy at free safety with a lot of range," Butler said. "But Eugene's got a lot of range. Now I can go up in the line and help the linebackers and linemen, and do some more aggressive stuff. We want to be unpredictable."

Together, they have indeed been that. And a lot more.

Frank Winters

He is from Hoboken, New Jersey. So automatically, you have to root for him.

Frank Winters, the Packers underrated and often overlooked center, is a throwback to the way football used to be played. He is happiest in the mud and dirt and the cold and blood. That's the game. At least that's how he played it in New Jersey.

For the last five seasons, after bouncing first from Cleveland to the New York Giants to Kansas City, Winters has found himself at home with the Packers.

Quite at home, in fact, since he has started 83 straight games, tying him for Green Bay's longest consecutive starting streak with running back Edgar Bennett.

It's a remarkable accomplishment, especially for a player who goes all out on every play as Winters does. Three seasons ago, he missed just one play all year.

"I think I got a neck stinger," Winters recalled. "Something like that. But I was back the next play."

And he's never left.

Winters rarely has gotten the credit he deserves, but the Packers, especially his best friend Brett Favre, know what he means to the offensive line.

Winters is the undisputed leader of the line. The guy with the most experience and the most fire. He is also one of the most versatile. Two years ago, injuries forced some juggling and Winters played 10 games at center and six at guard.

It was Winters' improved play in 1996, along with the rest of the line, that allowed the Packers' running game to kick into gear late in the season.

If there was one play Winters will remember, it came in the season finale against Minnesota. Blocking downfield on a screen pass, Winter popped Vikings cornerback Corey Fuller after the runner was down. Fuller took exception and poked Winters in the eye.

After the game Winters, sporting a nasty blood spot in his left eye, shrugged and said, "I never heard the whistle."

It was also a season that finally saw Winters get some well-deserved attention, as he was named to the NFC Pro Bowl team, the first Packer offensive lineman so honored since Larry McCarren in 1983.

Unfortunately for the 10-year veteran, the Super Bowl did not prove as wonderful as he'd hoped since, two days before the team was to leave for New Orleans, his older brother John died of heart complications.

After going back to New Jersey for the funeral, Winters joined the team and never missed a beat, playing every down in the victory.

Just as he always has.

Unfinished Business

December 22: Packers 38, Vikings 10

A S MUCH AS THERE WAS ON THE LINE FOR THE PACKERS IN THEIR SEASON finale, there was also this: good, old-fashioned, smelly revenge.

Yes, the Packers certainly wanted to win to lock up the home field through the playoffs. They knew only too well what a formidable weapon Lambeau Field in January could be.

Yes, they wanted to tie a franchise-best 13 victory record.

Yes, they wanted to win to maintain the momentum they'd built up over the past month.

But perhaps more than anything, they wanted to beat the Vikings because they were the Vikings. Next to the Dallas Cowboys, no team gets the Packers' blood pressure to spike the way the Vikings do. The history is turbulent enough and that normally would be plenty to keep the rivalry stoked.

And now a new dimension was added after the first meeting between the two teams Sept. 22 in the Metrodome. In that game, the Vikings had not only beaten the Packers physically, they'd embarrassed them.

Minnesota's mercury-quick defensive linemen had left Green Bay's offensive line grasping at air, and they sacked Brett Favre a career-worst seven times.

"We were awful," grumped right guard Adam Timmerman.

Also, the Packers had managed a season-low 217 yards and eight first downs on offense, and Minnesota handed Green Bay its first loss of the season.

All that was bad enough. What made it worse is the Vikings felt the need to tell the Packers all about it.

"I think it's pretty obvious we're the best team in the division," Minnesota linebacker Jeff Brady said at the time.

Now the Packers had a chance to make the Vikings eat their words.

After a rocky midseason, Minnesota pulled itself together behind quarterback Brad Johnson and earned a playoff berth.

So this would be the fifth straight Packer opponent playing without apparent motivation.

The Packers, on the other hand, were playing for everything.

"We want to beat those guys so bad," safety LeRoy Butler said. "We want to show them who is really the best team."

There were plenty of game-week fireworks as both sides hurled insults back and forth and Brady, who was cut by the Packers two years earlier, claimed he was going to tear Brett Favre's head off.

Fair to say that by Sunday, both sides were worked into a froth.

When all the talk ended and the game was played, some of the drama spilled away. The Packers made hash out of the Vikes, breaking open a 10-10 halftime stalemate with 28 unanswered points in the second half.

Thus the Packers finished the regular season with an 8-0 record at home. They had also won 16 in a row and 26 of their last 27 at Lambeau Field. More important, if anyone besides the Packers were going to represent the NFC in the Super Bowl, they'd have to come to Green Bay and whip the Packers in their sandbox.

That part of the mission was accomplished.

Tight end Keith Jackson acknowledges the Lambeau Field crowd after the Packers' resounding 38-10 win over the Vikings that clinched home-field advantage throughout the playoffs.

"A long time ago, I was telling a lot of people the road to the Super Bowl goes through here," Butler said. "I think I was proven right. Mike (Holmgren) told us one thing: If you're undefeated at home, you don't even have to worry about the Super Bowl. It'll come to you. That's what'll happen. Just think about being undefeated at home and everything else will work out itself."

And that's exactly what happened.

The Packers again were nothing to write home about in the first half, as they were outgained by the Vikings 193-155. If there was an ominous sign for Green Bay fans, it was that Favre again looked skittery against the Vikings pass rush, completing just 6 of 12 passes for 81 yards in the opening 30 minutes.

Ah, but by now the script was just repeating itself. As if by some weekly piece of magic, the Packers came out as a different team in the second half.

Howard returned the third-quarter kickoff 40 yards to the Packers 43. Six plays later, Favre threw a 13-yard touchdown pass to Dorsey Levens and the latest rout was on.

After a Minnesota punt, Favre roared right back, directing Green Bay on a nine-play, 76-yard march that chewed up 4:25. It ended appropriately as Favre threw a rocket to Andre Rison for the 22-yard touchdown.

Rison, who many thought was too undisciplined to play the game, had caught his first touchdown pass as a Packer and he did what all self-respecting Packers do – he leaped into the stands where he was engulfed by a sea of fans.

After another Viking punt, the relentless Favre kept up the pressure, driving Green Bay 61 yards in eight plays and hitting Keith

▲ **Cornerback Craig Newsome (21) exults after Eugene Robinson's wicked hit on Vikings' wide receiver Jake Reed. After giving up 309 yards against the Cowboys on Nov. 18, the Green Bay defense never allowed more than 292 yards the rest of the season.**

▲ Led by Brett Favre, the Packers return to their locker room victorious and in possession of the NFC's top seed in the play-offs.

Jackson for the 23-yard score. That touchdown was Favre's 39th scoring pass of the season, breaking the NFC mark of 38 he'd set the year before.

Favre's first touchdown of the year in Tampa had been to Jackson and now so had his final TD pass of the regular season – and in a matter of 15 minutes the Packers had blown open a tight game.

"He's Superman," Rison said of Favre. "He has no ego with his teammates, so we have great respect for him on the field. We'll do any task and take on any force that we have to for him."

Favre hit 15 of 23 passes for 202 yards and three touchdowns. For the season, he completed 60 percent of his passes for 3,899 yards, 39 touchdowns and only 13 interceptions.

As a team, the Packers became the first since the undefeated Miami Dolphins of 1972 to lead the league in most points scored (456) and fewest points allowed (210).

The defense was Green Bay's particular pride and joy.

The Packer defenders allowed just 19 touchdowns all season, breaking the record of 20 for a 16-game schedule (which began in 1978), set by the Chicago Bears in 1985.

Green Bay also finished the season as the NFL's top defense, allowing 4,156 yards, an average of just 260 per game.

"Without question, this is the best defense I've ever been around," defensive coordinator Fritz Shurmur said. "That's based on how they achieved, but it's also based on the fact that they're good people. These guys care about each other, about the coaches. They care about everything they do."

Said defensive end Sean Jones: "We've been playing so unselfishly all year. That (touchdown) stat right there is a true indicator of the team defense we've tried to play here. You think about 16 games and not giving up more than 19 touchdowns. That's an incredible feat.

▲ Coach Mike Holmgren reminds his team that while 13-3 is a fine regular season, the real work begins in the playoffs.

We're real proud of it."

But as remarkable as the Packers' regular season had been, every player knew the job wasn't finished.

"I think everybody knows what's at stake," Antonio Freeman said. "It's extremely tough to go 13-3 and we had the toughest schedule in the NFL. We were able to succeed in doing that and now the season's behind us. We're 0-0 now."

The playoff field was set.

In the NFC, the Vikings would travel to Dallas and the 49ers would host Philadelphia. The Carolina Panthers, in only their second year of existence, would have the other first-round bye.

Though the Packers knew their work was far from done, they also knew they'd have a week to heal up, relax and prepare for the playoffs.

"We going home for Christmas," Favre said. "And that's a great feeling."

It would only get better.

Chapter 6
Mud And Guts
January 4: Packers 35, 49ers 14

WHEN GREEN BAY PACKERS QUARTERBACK BRETT FAVRE awoke early Sunday morning and looked outside, the little butterflies in his stomach became B-52s. He could handle the cold if he had to. He could deal with the wind. He could even work with rain if it came to that.

But when Favre looked outside at what awaited him and the Packers that afternoon, he shook his head is dismay.

It was pouring. In Green Bay, in January and there was an honest to goodness Baptist downpour going on. On top of that, a steady, nasty wind had kicked up, dropping wind chills to nine degrees.

It was, in short, not exactly the ideal conditions in which to contest an NFC division championship game. Especially when it concerned the San Francisco 49ers.

As Favre watched the rain pelt down, he decided he'd make the best of a bad situation. What choice did he have?

Defensive tackle Santana Dotson was wide awake at 4:30 a.m. and, try as he might, he could not get back to sleep. Too many thoughts running through his head about the game to come. Too much to think about. Too much to deal with if they lost.

He wondered about the Packers' marvelous 13-3 season and how empty everyone would feel if they fell short in the playoffs.

It was too awful to think about.

"I heard the rain coming down," Dotson said. "Then I decided this was Lambeau weather, Green Bay weather, so I might as well go out and have some fun with it."

Andre Rison was up early, too.

He knew he was about to play the most significant game in his eight-year career. And he knew he could play a pivotal role.

Rison had been to the playoffs before with Atlanta, but the Falcons had been little more than window dressing, a team to fill out the bracket.

This was different. This team felt different. This team acted different. This team was different. And though he'd been a part of it for barely two months, he already felt like he belonged as a Packer.

"This is a team," Rison said. "This group of guys make up a team and not too many people in the National Football League can say they actually have a team."

The time had come for the Green Bay Packers.

Since training camp in July, they had talked about this moment, this time, this circumstance. They had talked about the

After spending much of the season as a backup on the offensive line, 10-year veteran Bruce Wilkerson received a huge surprise prior to Green Bay's finale against Minnesota. Realizing that the playoffs were a time for veteran leadership, Mike Holmgren inserted Wilkerson at left tackle and the Packers never missed a beat.

▶ The expression of linebacker Brian Williams said all that needed to be said about the horrendous weather the Packers and 49ers had to slog around in during the divisional playoff game at Lambeau Field.

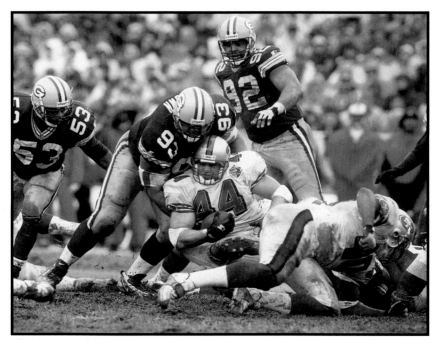

▲ Nose tackle Gilbert Brown demonstrates to San Francisco fullback Tommy Vardell that it was pointless to run up the middle on the Packers.

▲ Cornerback Doug Evans wraps up the always dangerous 49ers receiver Jerry Rice. The Packers beat San Francisco in part because the defense shut down Rice with only five catches for just 36 yards.

horrible feeling they took away from the NFC title game in Dallas the previous season, when they were 10 minutes from the Super Bowl and let it all slip away.

They talked about how that was not going to happen again. That this season would be different. That when presented with the opportunity to excel, they would not hesitate a moment.

It had all come down to this.

The Packers had battled through some oppressive setbacks during a season that included injuries to key members of the offense. They had taken on the NFL's toughest schedule, including two three-game road trips – which no NFL team had done in 20 years. They played all comers and they had pulled through impressively with a 13-3 record as the team to beat in the NFC and, by definition, all of pro football.

Here was rarified air indeed for a franchise that as recently as two years earlier, could not be taken very seriously.

Now it was all spread before them like some great feast. They had set some lofty goals heading into the season and they had attained them all – repeat championship in the NFC Central Division; the conference's best record; home-field advantage throughout the playoffs.

They had it all. Now came the time to find out if they could handle it.

Oh, the Packers understood well enough that the journey was fraught with potential peril. First they would face the 49ers, a team that knew the Packers almost as well as the Packers knew themselves. And this was a 49er team bent on serious revenge after absorbing two losses to Green Bay in less than a year.

If the Pack managed to survive the 49ers, either the Carolina Panthers or the Dallas Cowboys awaited in the NFC title game.

And in that one, it was a question of the devil you knew or the devil you didn't know.

Green Bay fans desperately wanted the Cowboys, especially in Lambeau Field. They could almost picture the 'Boys slipping and sliding all over the frozen field while the Packers exacted the kind of retribution generally found in the Old Testament.

For Packers fans, a good old-fashioned Wisconsin whipping would go a long way toward healing the wounds of seven straight losses to the Cowboys, including three in the playoffs.

On the other hand, they knew next to nothing about the Panthers, an expansion team in just its second year.

It was a team on the rise, with a rocket-armed quarterback in Kerry Collins, an offense that made few mistakes and a defense that could be troublesome. Other than that, they were an enigma.

That's what waited down the road. In front of the Packers, though, were the 49ers, who still weren't convinced the Packers were for real.

"Everybody's ready to hand the Super Bowl to the Packers," sniffed Niners tight end Brent Jones. "They haven't won anything yet."

The Packers had to agree. Until they won the big games in the pressure situations, they would be nothing more than lovable under-achievers.

Now, in the muck and the mire and mud of Lambeau Field, the Packers had their chance.

The story all week had been the health of San Francisco quarterback Steve Young. In a wild-card playoff game the week before against Philadelphia in rainy San Francisco, Young had taken a wicked hit to the ribs while running for a touchdown.

He remained in the game and helped orchestrate the 49er win that set up this rematch in Green Bay. But clearly Young was not himself.

During the week, Young kept insisting he'd play against the Packers and that his bruised ribs would not be a significant problem. As soon as Young stepped on the raw, wet field in Green Bay, though, it became obvious those ribs were a serious hindrance.

On the game's first series, Young ran for three yards, wincing all the way to the sideline. On third down, he threw a poor pass to Jerry Rice that fell incomplete.

It was only after the game that Young admitted his bruised ribs were actually cracked, and that no amount of padding or medication was going to make up for the fact that he simply couldn't play effectively.

"He had two broken ribs, but he couldn't tell anybody because it would have put a big target on him," Jones said.

Knowing the importance of the game,

◄ Brett Favre doing what he does best, scrambling away from a pass rush. In the deluge, Favre played a smart, controlled game, throwing for just 79 yards (but with no turnovers) and letting the running game take over.

▲ Desmond Howard embarks on his 71-yard punt return that set the tone early for this playoff game.

▲ Desmond Howard slips through the Niners line on his way to returning another punt 46 yards, setting up Green Bay's second touchdown. "He made the difference early," Brett Favre said. "He may have been the difference all day."

▶ Desmond Howard crosses the goal line after scoring on the 71-yard punt return.

Young wanted to take the chance and play, but he and coach George Seifert knew right away that it was a mistake.

"If it wasn't my throwing side, it would've been all right," Young said. "But it was my throwing side. It's like a knife in your back. When I'd try to throw a 'go' or air it out, then I'd feel it."

Even Seifert admitted it was a mistake to even activate Young for the game.

But it was too late anyway.

After that first series. San Francisco punted to the dangerous Howard, whose effectiveness figured to be negated in the quagmire. That turned out to be a poor assumption.

Howard gathered in the punt at his own 29 and took off.

"It was a very returnable kick," Howard said. "I just tried to take it up the middle. It was kind of like a blur after that. I remember seeing 33 (Dedrick Dodge) on my right, so I wanted to cut up inside of him. Then I saw 50 (Gary Plummer) and I made a move to my left on him. At that point there was nothing but the punter."

Still, Howard displayed remarkable footing on the sloppy track while would-be 49ers tacklers flopped around like goldfish on a basement floor.

The 71-yard touchdown return not only gave Green Bay a quick 7-0 lead, it was the first break in a game that surely would hinge on which team got the most.

"Desmond made the difference in the game early," coach Mike Holmgren said.

Howard wasn't quite finished, either.

Five minutes later, Howard again got great blocking and made several tacklers miss. This time he hauled a punt 46 yards to the 49er 7-yard line before he was tripped up with a shoe-top tackle by Frankie Smith.

Two plays after Howard's dash, Favre threw a bullet to Rison, who hung on in the end zone despite being drilled by safety Tim McDonald.

Barely five minutes into the game, the Packers were on top 14-0. They could not have scripted it any better.

"(Howard's) returns definitely made a difference early in the game," Favre said. "It may have made the difference all day. It set the tone."

Green Bay eventually expanded its lead to 21-0 in the second quarter, thanks to a Craig

Newsome interception of relief quarterback Elvis Grbac at the 49ers 15.

Three plays after that, Edgar Bennett sloshed into the end zone for the 2-yard touchdown that seemed to signal that the rout was on.

But it wasn't.

As quickly as the breaks had gone the Packers' way, they suddenly shifted directions late in the second quarter.

The Packers defense had held the Niners once again and Tommy Thompson – aiming away from Howard by this time – punted to the left sideline, where Packer blockers Tyrone Williams and Chris Hayes were working. The ball skidded off the unsuspecting Hayes and San Francisco's Curtis Buckley fell on it at the Green Bay 26.

"It was just one of those things," Hayes said. "We were really trying to focus and concentrate on blocking Buckley, and getting him out of the way. It was a bad break."

The turnover produced points, as Grbac hit Terry Kirby for the 8-yard touchdown with just 32 seconds left in the half.

Things got even dicier at the start of the third quarter, and a wardrobe change had a lot to do with it.

Most of the Packers, including Howard, seized the opportunity to completely ditch their soaked and muddy uniforms for fresh duds during the halftime break. But Howard had taken a little longer than the others and was unaware that the rest of the team had left for the field to start the second half.

"I had to get some dry stuff," Howard said. "I couldn't stop shivering on the bench, and I knew I couldn't be effective like that."

Don Beebe took his usual deep spot on the kickoff return unit, but quickly realized something was wrong. Desmond was missing.

"I probably should've just called a timeout," Beebe said.

Instead, Rison tried to make a late save, and came sprinting onto the field to take Howard's vacated spot – even though he hadn't played on special teams in years.

The kickoff subsequently came up short and squirted past Beebe.

"The ball just hit and scooted," Beebe said. "I'm not sure if it went right, left or between my legs."

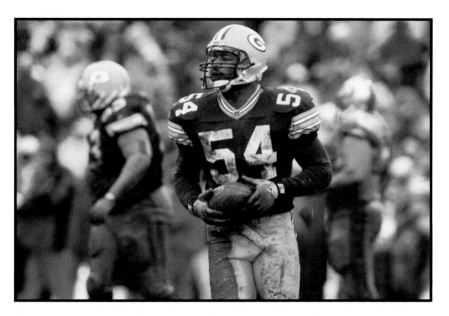

▲ **Ron Cox was a free agent from the Bears who came to Green Bay thinking the starting middle lineacking job was his. But when George Koonce was moved to the middle, Cox quietly played the backup role. When Koonce was hurt against the 49ers, Cox came in and played superbly.**

▲ **George Koonce, the Packers' leading tackler, celebrates Green Bay's victory. But his joy would be short-lived as he learned soon after that he'd suffered a knee injury and would miss the rest of the playoffs.**

▲ Safety Eugene Robinson intercepted two Elvis Grbac passes to snuff out potential 49er rallies.

▶ Halfback Edgar Bennett, who hates being called a great bad-weather runner, nonetheless proved it again by rushing for 80 yards and two touchdowns in horrible conditions.

Where it did go was into the arms of San Francisco's Steve Israel, who fell on the thing at the Packer 4-yard line.

Grbac then used a great play fake and rolled into the end zone for the score that pulled the Niners within 21-14 and it appeared the Packers might be self-destructing.

Howard was walking out of the team tunnel just as the ball was kicked off and he knew right away he had a penthouse in the coach's doghouse.

"I felt for Desmond, really," Beebe said. "That's got to be such an empty feeling knowing, 'Oh God, we just had a kick return and I'm supposed to be out there.' "

It was suddenly a game again – or so it looked.

In fact, the Green Bay offense was prepared to stop the nonsense immediately. On the ensuing drive, the Packers showed they indeed had the stuff to be champions, marching 72 yards in 12 plays while using up nearly eight minutes.

On that drive, Favre threw only two passes, the longest an 18-yarder to Antonio Freeman to the San Francisco 7.

Other than that, Bennett did most of the work, rushing five times for 29 yards. Bennett would have had a touchdown if he hadn't been cracked at the goal line by safety Merton Hanks, whereupon the usually surehanded Bennett fumbled.

Fortunately, Freeman was right on the spot and dove on the ball for the touchdown.

"It seemed like there were 20 guys on me," Freeman said. "But all I remember is Brett and (center) Frankie Winters saying, 'Hang in there, Free, hang in there.' "

Freeman did and the Packers had their two-touchdown cushion restored. They never lost it again.

From there, the defense simply took over.

The 49ers did threaten one last time, as they drove to the Green Bay 19 early in the fourth quarter, but linebacker Brian Williams forced a William Floyd fumble that he also recovered at the 17.

On the next series, Mike Prior forced Kirby to fumble a punt that Hayes scooped up at the 49er 32. Six plays after that, Bennett swept right from the 11 and scored. At that point, the Packers could begin celebrating a thorough, convincing win over one of the NFL's glamor franchises.

It was a workmanlike effort for Green Bay, as Favre threw just 15 passes, equalling the fewest ever he'd thrown as a Packer in games he'd started and finished. Favre completed 11 for a mere 79 yards, the fewest ever for a Holmgren-coached team.

The running game made the difference, as Bennett rushed 17 times for 90 yards and Dorsey Levens added 46 yards on 15 carries.

The Packers gained 210 total yards overall, 139 coming on the ground. More accurately, in the mud.

"The running just flat took over this game," Bennett said.

And Bennett, who is often referred to as a "mudder" – to his eternal annoyance – got much of the credit.

"You've got to understand something," safety LeRoy Butler said. "Edgar's the best bad-weather running back in the league, so he was hoping it would rain a little more."

"If he played for somebody else, everybody would think the world of him," Rison said. "(Edgar's) one of my unsung heroes. To me, he's one of the best backs in football."

So the Packers had cleared their first hurdle. And it was especially sweet coming against the 49ers, the aging dowager still reluctant to hand over the throne.

"I think we deserve respect now, the respect the 49ers weren't giving us," tight end Mark Chmura said. "I never heard a quote coming out of their locker room saying that we were a good team. All we heard was that they didn't have so-and-so playing, and I'm sure they're going to say something like that now. But beating them three times in one year? You tell me. I think it offended a lot of guys in this locker room. They're a good team and we'll admit they are. But I think we are too."

Freeman was asked if the win represented a changing of the guard in the NFL.

"Hopefully," he said. "Today we took a step. But nobody here thinks we're invincible. We're a football team on a mission. We like our chances. I think that's a better word."

▼Images in the mud: Defensive end Reggie White; right guard Adam Timmerman; right tackle Earl Dotson.

Nothing Could Be Finer

NFC Championship
January 12: Packers 30, Panthers 13

N AND OF ITSELF, THE FIELD WAS NOTHING SPECIAL.

It was grass and dirt, like a million other football fields in a million other places.

There were no magical properties.

The stadium? Green corrugated metal, surrounding 60,000 or so metal bleachers that were hot in the summer and cold in the winter.

Driving down Lombardi Avenue, you see it rising above the riot of fast-food burger joints and bakeries and grocery store signs like some greenish Rock of Gibraltar.

As one of the older venues in the NFL, the place is home to ghosts and myths and legends.

Oh my, does Lambeau Field have those.

What the stadium lacks in modern conveniences, it more than makes up for in sheer history.

In this place, Paul Hornung, Bart Starr, Jerry Kramer, Fuzzy Thurston and other legends played the game better than anyone of their day. And on the sidelines prowled Vince Lombardi, still considered the best coach the league has ever seen and still spoken of in reverential tones in these parts.

The spirits live here, there is little doubt of that. And they live because coach Mike Holmgren summoned them one night with some bizarre West Coast incantation.

It is to the point now where the Green Bay Packers can step on their Lambeau Field turf and know deep in their souls that they will not, cannot, be beaten in their own house.

"The players just feel that," Holmgren said. "They really believe that no one can come in here and beat them."

The conviction took shape on a cool Sunday night – October 10, 1993 – when the Packers held off a late Denver rally to win 30-27. That triumph ended a three-game losing streak and helped Green Bay stay on course to its first playoff berth in 10 years.

Since that time, the Packers had lost exactly once at Lambeau Field, when they were ambushed in the 1995 season opener by the St. Louis Rams, 17-14.

After that sneak attack by the Rams, the Packers reeled off 17 straight at home, the best mark in football.

In 1996, they raced through their home schedule with a glittering 8-0 regular-season mark and a 35-14 playoff spanking of the tradition-rich 49ers the week before.

And this was why the Packers had fought so hard for the NFC's best record, so they could assure themselves the home field in the playoffs. Because to their way of thinking, they felt as close to invincible in Lambeau Field as any team could feel without being armed with nuclear weapons.

"The home-field advantage is every-

▶ Dorsey Levens runs away from the pack on his way 66 yards downfield with a Brett Favre screen pass. On the next play, Edgar Bennett blasted into the end zone from four yards out to give Green Bay a 27-13 lead and putting the Super Bowl glimmer in everyone's eyes. (Photo by Scott Cunningham)

▲ The Lambeau Field scoreboard reveals the frozen facts about the NFC Championship Game.

▲ With the Packers preparing to play in wind-chills of 19-below, the Packers equipment staff prepares a bunch of heat packs to keep the players' hands warm.

thing," Holmgren said simply.

Now the Packers could put that theory to its ultimate test as they faced the upstart Carolina Panthers in the NFC title game.

A bit of housekeeping came first, however. The Packers wouldn't have that home-field advantage until they could produce an actual field. The miserable weather for the 49er game left Lambeau's turf ruined, and it had to be replaced in less than a week.

Perhaps only in the skewed and strange world of pro sports could a groundskeeper become a media star. But that was the case with Todd Edelbeck, Lambeau's head groundskeeper.

NFL officials took a look at what passed for a football field on the Monday after that San Francisco mud bath and decided that it would not do, especially for a game that would decide a Super Bowl berth.

So the league invested $150,000 to have 40 trucks of Maryland sod transported to Green Bay for a major re-sodding project. And it would be conducted under the auspices of Edelbeck and Chip Toma, the NFL's field and turf consultant.

In a slightly bizarre scenario, Edelbeck, a quiet fellow with muddy boots and a bemused expression, was hauled up on the Packers auditorium stage to answer a barrage of questions from the nation's media.

Edelbeck acquitted himself well.

The groundskeeper made it clear that the intent was not to grow new grass, a virtual impossibility at that time of year in Green Bay, but to pack it together tightly enough to hold for one game.

Each roll of sod weighed 2,000 pounds and was 42 feet long by 42 inches wide, and it would take an army of volunteers and professional sod-layers to get the job done in time.

But there was no other choice.

"It's just something we need to do to make this field ready for the game," Edelbeck said. "Right now, the field's in poor shape. Not to the point where we couldn't bring it back, but I think we want to do the best we possibly can for this game."

The task required digging up what was left of the field and starting fresh. It was a great opportunity for local charities as the Packers donation of turf, sold as "Frozen Tundra," raised over $200,000.

The tundra sold out in four hours.

By Thursday, it became apparent that Edelbeck and his crew had performed something akin to a miracle. Several Packer coaches even poked their heads out to see how it was proceeding and were impressed.

"The field's going to be in good shape," offensive coordinator Sherm Lewis said. "The field is not going to be a factor."

The Panthers? They were another story.

Though the Packers had gone bleary-eyed studying tape of their foe, nothing replaced facing a team in live combat. And these teams never had met.

Here's what the Packers did know: The week before, the Panthers, in their first-ever playoff game, had hosted the defending Super Bowl champion Dallas Cowboys and mugged them.

Whatever else the Packers knew, they knew that Carolina had done to Dallas what they had been unable to do in their last seven meetings. And that alone was cause for serious respect.

Offensively, second-year quarterback Kerry Collins had played like a seasoned veteran, making just enough good plays to keep the Cowboys off-balance. He didn't throw much, but the passes he needed were on target and came at the right times. Meanwhile, tailback Anthony Johnson shredded the Cowboys for more than 100 yards.

But it was the Carolina defense which had the Packers truly concerned.

Coached by defensive wizard Dom Capers, the Panthers employed an exotic zone blitz that featured linebackers swarming in from anywhere on the field. Carolina's schemes forced quarterbacks to make instantaneous decisions about who was coming and from where – if anyone was coming at all.

If executed properly, the idea of a blitz is just as deadly as the actual blitz and it forces quarterbacks into bad decisions.

The Panthers had caused havoc with Cowboys quarterback Troy Aikman and forced a late interception that ended a possible Dallas comeback.

The Panthers' victory had sent Packers fans into a black depression. After all, they had dreamed of getting the Cowboys in Lambeau

◄ Dorsey Levens had the game of his life against the Panthers, rushing for 88 yards on 10 carries and catching five passes for 117 more yards.

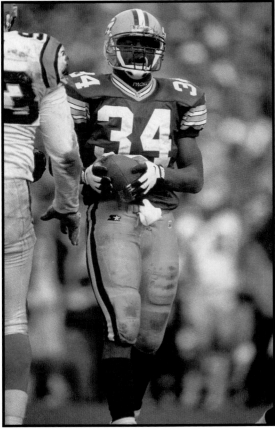

◄ Edgar Bennett also had a great game, rushing 25 times for 99 yards and scoring the critical touchdown.

▶ The old and the new get together prior to the game as ex-Packers great, Hall of Famer Paul Hornung, and Brett Favre talk before the coin toss.

▲ Packers coach Mike Holmgren shows Carolina coach Dom Capers the best place to keep warm at Lambeau Field. Though the temperature plummeted to well-below zero wind-chills, the weather never really was a factor in the game.

for a game that really mattered and then dispensing their version of justice.

It was a sentiment the Panthers understood.

"I know Packers fans wanted the Cowboys," Collins said. "I understand that completely because it's become such a great rivalry. But you know what? We beat the Cowboys and we're here."

Packers defensive end Reggie White said the Panthers were no surprise to them.

"A lot of us thought Carolina would beat the Cowboys," White said. "I know I did. They're a good team and they deserve to be here."

As the field rounded into shape, the Packers got another bit of good news. The weather, which had surprised them the week before, was back to its old self.

The forecast for game day was perfect: sunny, 7 degrees and wind chills near 30 below.

Now that was a home-field advantage, especially for quarterback Brett Favre who, inexplicably was 18-0 in home games played under 35 degrees. Not bad for a guy from balmy Mississippi.

"I can't explain it," Favre said, "because I hate this stuff."

Naturally, both sides shrugged off the topic of cold weather.

"I don't think it matters," Holmgren said. "I like games that are decided on the field and not by the elements, and I hope that's the case here."

Carolina linebacker Sam Mills tried to put an even better spin on it.

"It got cold in Charlotte this week," he said. "It actually got down to around freezing, so I think that will help us. Besides, it's going to be cold for both teams."

Finally, the game arrived and 60,216 fans (there were only 574 no-shows) were on hand to witness what they hoped would be a bit of history. A victory would give the Packers their first-ever NFC title and a trip back to the Super Bowl after a 29-year absence.

Both teams started tentatively, as Carolina picked up one first down on its opening possession and the Packers got two. Carolina again failed to move on its next possession but Rohn Stark's punt pinned the Packers back on their own 6.

On first down, a skitterish Favre, keeping an eye out for that blitz he knew was coming sooner or later, nearly threw an interception to cornerback Tyrone Poole.

On second down, Favre was just as bad but not as fortunate.

Favre tried to thread a pass to Don Beebe on a slant pattern, but Mills stepped in front and intercepted it, returning the ball to the Green Bay 2.

After the pick, Panthers All-Pro linebacker Lamar Lathon went up to Favre and said ominously, "It's going to be a long day."

"What could I say?" Favre recalled later. "If I kept making plays like that, he was right."

Following Mills' interception, Collins used a great play fake and threw a touchdown pass to an embarrassingly wide-open Howard Griffith, quieting the crowd and handing Carolina a 7-0 lead.

The Packers continued to sputter, drawing penalties on two straight plays before driving to the Panthers 28, where Chris Jacke's 46-yard

◄ Andre Rison made his presence felt against the Panthers gambling, blitzing defense. He caught three passes for 53 yards, including a big 22-yarder that set up a Green Bay touchdown.

▲ The picture says it all as mist rises off the frozen field.

▶ After throwing a first-quarter interception deep in his own territory that led to Carolina's first touchdown, Brett Favre gets an earful from Panthers linebacker Lamar Lathon. "He told me It's going to be long day," Favre said. "And if I kept making throws like that, he was going to be right." (Photo by Chris Dennis)

▲ Perhaps the turning point of the game. Dorsey Levens comes down with a touch-down pass despite the best efforts of cor-nerback Eric Davis. The 29-yard strike from Favre tied the game and helped turn the momentum back to Green Bay. (Photo by Chris Dennis)

field goal attempt fell short.

"We knew if we could hang around, we could make a game of it," Collins said.

And Carolina was doing more than that.

Finally, the tide turned in Green Bay's favor and the momentum switch was provided by an unlikely source.

Dorsey Levens had accepted his role as Edgar Bennett's backup at tailback. All Levens wanted, as every Packer did, was a chance to contribute, a chance to prove he could help the cause.

And Levens had done that in recent weeks, giving Green Bay's rushing game a badly need-ed boost. On this championship Sunday, though, he had a chance to be the hero.

The Packers started a drive late in the first quarter and seemed in danger of sparking out again when they faced third and one on their own 36.

But Levens burst off right tackle and powered 35 yards to the Carolina 29.

Then on the first snap of the second quarter, Levens split wide right and was matched up with Pro Bowl cornerback Eric Davis. This was a play Holmgren planned to run several times and one he told his team earlier in the week would result in a touchdown.

Favre rolled right, waited for Levens to slip past Davis and then lofted a pass toward the corner of the end zone that the 240-pound Levens leaped to snatch away from Davis.

Touchdown.

"It was unusual because it was a running back, but it's not unusual because it was Dorsey," wide receiver Antonio Freeman said. "He's a fantastic athlete. He's an unselfish guy. He waited for the opportunity and he made the best of it. He was a huge spark for us."

Even though the Packers had tied the game, it was far from over. As Collins had asked, the Panthers were hanging around.

On Green Bay's next series, Favre was flushed from the pocket and was being chased by defensive end Mike Fox when he simply fumbled the ball. Lathon recovered at the Green Bay 45.

"I just dropped it," Favre said. "It was kind of embarrassing. I thought I was done with those kinds of plays, but apparently, I'm not."

The Panthers took partial advantage of the mistake, moving to the Green Bay 4 before the defense stiffened, forced two Collins incompletions and made Carolina settle for John Kasay's field goal and a 10-7 lead.

That's probably when the Packers decided enough was enough.

Holding the ball for nearly eight minutes, Green Bay steadily marched from its own 29 to the Carolina 6. Along the way, the Packers converted on two third downs and on the biggest play of the drive, Favre drilled a laser to Andre Rison for 22 yards.

On the next play, Favre threw a perfect timing pass to Freeman, who beat Poole to the corner of the end zone for a touchdown with 48 seconds remaining in the half.

And the Packers weren't done.

Remember all those wild first-half finishes during the regular season? Green Bay was due for one in the playoffs.

◄ Favre's second, and last, big mistake came in the second quarter when he dropped the ball while scrambling and Lamar Lathon recovered. Carolina got a field goal, and a 10-7 lead, out of it. (Photo by Scott Cunningham)

▼ Chris Jacke prepares to boot a 31-yard field goal that put the Packers up, 17-10, late in the second quarter. Jacke kicked field goals of 31, 32 and 28 yards.

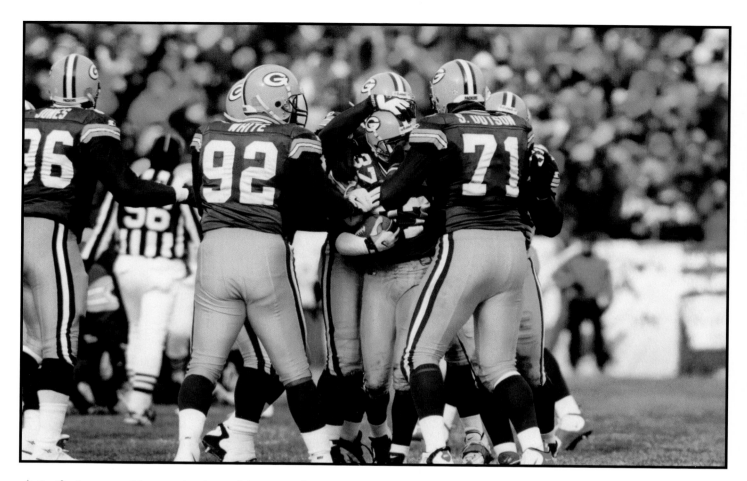

▲ In that mass of humanity is rookie cornerback Tyrone Williams (37), whose spectacular diving, one-handed interception late in the first half set up a Green Bay field goal. (Photo by Chris Dennis)

▲ Second-year cornerback Craig Newsome played an exceptional game against the Panthers. Though he was beaten early on a long pass, he came back to finish with six tackles, three pass defenses and an interception that sealed Carolina's fate. (Photo by Chris Dennis)

On Carolina's first play after the Freeman touchdown, Collins tried to go deep down the left sideline to Willie Green, but rookie cornerback Tyrone Williams made a diving, one-handed interception at the Packer 38.

Favre then threw 23 yards to Rison and 25 more to Freeman, and Jacke kicked a 31-yard field goal to give Green Bay a 17-10 halftime lead.

The halftime statistics were scary, from either viewpoint.

Green Bay dominated the opening half, out-gaining the Panthers 271-103, including a massive 121-13 edge in rushing yardage. But those two key Favre mistakes had kept the Panthers in the game.

That was the Carolina game plan. Hang around.

But in the second half, they couldn't.

As the Packers had done so often all season, they took the second half kickoff with the intention of cutting somebody's heart out.

This time, it was an 11-play drive that took 6:44 off the clock and put the Panthers back against the ropes one more time.

Two plays were critical to that drive. The first came on third down and three from the Green Bay 17, when Favre hit Beebe on a crossing pattern for 29 yards to the Packer 46.

Then on third and seven from the Carolina 32, Favre appeared to be dead, caught in the clutches of Pro Bowl linebacker Kevin Greene. But as he was going down, Favre shoveled a pass to a waiting Levens, who gained eight yards and kept the drive alive.

All Greene could say after that play was, "Wow."

"You know how Brett is," Packers defensive end Sean Jones said. "Brett can do a myriad of things and sometimes they don't work out. But he's always going to make it right in the end."

And so he did in this instance.

After that miracle throw to Levens, the Packers picked up nine more yards before the drive stalled and Jacke knocked down a 32-yard field goal to make it 20-10.

The heart wasn't quite cut out, but there was blood loss.

Carolina kept plugging away, driving 73 yards in 11 plays and reaching the Packer 5 before that drive fell apart and Kasay had to kick a 23-yard field goal.

At that point, the Panthers trailed 20-13 and still had a pulse. They had done all they had hoped to do, staying in the game and hoping to cash in on one big Packers mistake.

Instead, Levens provided what would prove to be the knockout blow.

The Packers started their next drive on their 26 and Bennett picked up four yards to the 30. Then came the key play of the game and possibly the season.

Sensing a blitz was coming, Favre lofted a screen pass to Levens over the outstretched arms of Greene in the right flat. Levens then cut inside safety Pat Terrell, got a nice block from center Frank Winters and ran 66 yards down the right sideline to the Carolina 4.

"Once I made that one cutback and the linemen picked those guys up, it opened up," Levens said.

On the next play, Bennett slashed off right

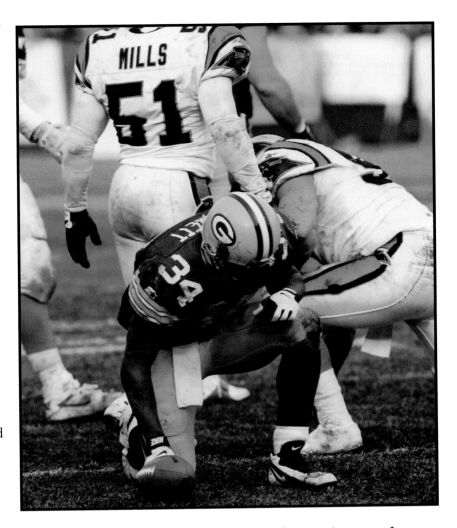

▲ Edgar Bennett offers a silent prayer after scoring on a four-yard run that all but sent the Packers winging to New Orleans. (Photo Chris Dennis)

▲ Tyrone Williams and Chris Hayes celebrate on the sidelines after Green Bay's win.

▲ Sean Jones gives coach Mike Holmgren the traditional victory bath, this time dumping a bucket of ice on the coach's head. "It was, well, cold," Holmgren said, smiling. "But it felt great."

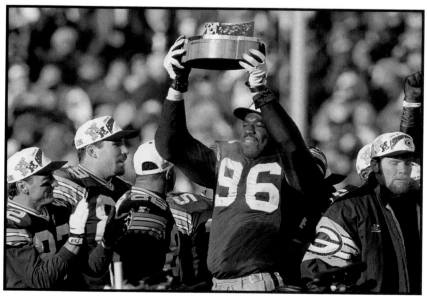

▲ Sean Jones shows off the George Halas Trophy, given to the NFC champs, to the delirious crowd at Lambeau Field.

guard untouched for the touchdown that gave Green Bay a 27-13 cushion and the Super Bowl at least was in sight.

Levens ended up playing the game of his life when the Packers needed it the most. He rushed for a career-best 88 yards on only 10 carries and tossed in five receptions for 117 yards, another career high.

"I thought I would contribute a little bit, but I never dreamed of having a game like this," he said. "This is definitely a career game for me. I don't know if I was waiting for (something like this), but I'm always confident I can help the team. I'm in the game plan every week. Usually not this much, though."

After Bennett's touchdown, the Panthers began to unravel.

Two plays later, tailback Anthony Johnson

fumbled and LeRoy Butler recovered at the Panther 47. Green Bay then drove to the Carolina 11, where Jacke kicked his third field goal – from 28 yards out – and the big celebration was coming.

In the final minute of the game, as the Lambeau Field crowd surged and rolled and screamed, Favre left the field to an ovation and immediately leaped into the arms of Reggie White.

"This was for you," Favre whispered to White, who had not won a championship at any level in any sport in his life.

At last, Reggie's dream was coming true. He was going to the Super Bowl.

Also in the final minute, general manager Ron Wolf was watching, his eyes ablaze with emotion.

"This makes it all worthwhile, doesn't it?" someone asked him.

"Damn right it does," Wolf roared, and he proceeded to wave his arms and whip the crowd into a further frenzy. "How about those Packers?" Wolf screamed to the crowd.

On the awards podium afterward, Holmgren, Wolf and team president Bob Harlan were joined by as many of the Packers as could fit on the thing without it collapsing under the strain.

And despite the bitter temperatures, no one in the crowd left. They stayed to soak it all in.

For Harlan, this was a particularly emotional moment. He had been with the team for 26 years and seen the once-proud franchise fall into mediocrity.

Harlan also was the one who was eating lunch with New York Giants owner George Young five years ago and talking about how concerned he was about the Packers and where they were or were not going.

That was the point where Harlan made the decision to the pull the trigger and hire Ron Wolf away from the New York Jets and give him carte blanche to turn the Packers around.

Wolf's first move was to hire Holmgren. His second was to steal Brett Favre away from the Atlanta Falcons.

The rest, as they say, is history.

So there, on a crystal clear, frozen afternoon, it had all come to pass. And Harlan was crying.

"No way in the world did I expect this," Harlan said after the awards ceremony. "I was so nervous this week. It's been a very upsetting week and I'm just so delighted now. To reach this game means the world to me."

Then he shook his head in wonder and utter amazement.

"Thank God Ron Wolf and Mike Holmgren came to Green Bay," Harlan said softly.

On the field, the Packers didn't want the

▲ Reggie White salutes the Packers faithful after beating Carolina. (Photo by Scott Cunningham)

▲ **Receivers coach Gil Haskell, right, talks to Mike Reinfeldt, the Packers chief financial officer, after the game. A year ago, Haskell was in a Texas hospital recovering from a severe head injury suffered when he slammed into the artifical turf at Texas Stadium after a play. Though he was seriously ill for several weeks, Haskell made a complete recovery and was back coaching in time for training camp.**

group hug to end. Several players leaped into the stands, others waved to the crowd and Reggie White skipped around Lambeau Field like a five-year-old on the playground.

And as the Packers reveled in their victory, the Panthers watched in silent respect. They'd been whipped and they knew it. At that moment, they understood what the Packers had known all along, that the value of having the home field in the playoffs cannot be measured.

"The home-field advantage is key," Carolina tight end Wesley Walls said. "That's something we're going to set our sights on next year. The Packers' crowd was into it, along with the whole town."

"The home-field advantage goes to the best team and that was the case today," Carolina general manager Bill Polian said. "It was no fluke. The Packers showed that today on the field. If you want to be the best, you have to do the things that it takes to be the best."

Inside the locker room, though, many of the Packers reacted to their title with a kind of numb acceptance.

"I expected to be doing cartwheels out there today," Antonio Freeman said. "I know we're going to the Super Bowl, but I don't think the reality of the matter has set in yet. I'm not upset. I'm not crying. The Super Bowl was our goal and now we're there."

But this was special for three veterans in particular – White, Sean Jones, Eugene Robinson – who combined had played 37 NFL seasons without a title among them.

"God always has the last laugh," said White, who took his share of criticism four years ago when he signed as a free agent with the Packers. "It was all in Jesus' plan. People around the country can laugh all they want, but this was all His plan."

For Robinson, who spent 11 seasons in

Seattle without getting close to a Super Bowl, this was the capper to a great career.

"We had some good teams in Seattle," he said, "but I don't know if it was chemistry, not pulling it together. We were always kind of behind the eight-ball, always digging holes for ourselves. Here, we're not digging holes for ourselves. We're trying to go out and seize the moment."

Jones might have been the most emotional of all.

"I started losing faith a few times in Houston," he said. "I never thought I'd get another opportunity because we blew so many opportunities in Houston. I'm just so overwhelmed and so blessed to have gotten another opportunity."

But the job was not finished.

All the goals the Packers had set for themselves this season had fallen like snowflakes.

But there was still one more task to be completed – Super Bowl XXXI at the Louisiana Superdome against another upstart, the New England Patriots.

For Favre, here was the game he had always dreamed about, playing in a Super Bowl an hour from his home in Hancock County, Mississippi.

And though two weeks of staggering hype awaited, the Packers were looking forward to it. After all, it had taken 29 years to get back.

"I'm not worried about tickets (for family), I'm not worried about anything," Favre said. "It sure beats the alternative, I can assure you of that."

EVERYWHERE THE GREEN BAY PACKERS TURN, THEY ARE SURROUNDED BY tradition.

From Lombardi Avenue to Lambeau Field to Packerland Avenue to Lombardi Middle School to the Packers Hall of Fame directly across the street from the stadium, Green Bay is steeped in history and the celebration of the Packers' glorious accomplishments.

While some might call it an obsession with the past, for years it was all the city, the region — and the state of Wisconsin, for that matter — could hang a hat on.

So as Packer teams struggled in mediocrity for a couple of decades, fans continued to sing the praises of the old-timers who delivered five championships (including the first two Super Bowls) over a seven-year span from 1961 through 1967.

Mike Holmgren was hit face-first with that tradition when he joined the Packers in 1992. He knew that every Green Bay head coach since the sainted Vince Lombardi had a progressively worse winning percentage.

From Phil Bengston to Dan Devine to Bart Starr to Forrest Gregg to Lindy Infante, the Packers had simply gotten worse and worse.

"I knew about the Green Bay Packers and I knew about coach Lombardi," Holmgren said. "I was one of those kids growing up, when I was in junior high and high school (in San Francisco) playing foot-

ball and so on, I was really a sponge and I read everything I could on everybody in the league. I could give you who played on what team and all that kind of stuff. So I was very much aware of the history and the tradition of the team."

"What I have learned and I didn't know, even though I knew a lot about the team, is the people, and the area, and the state. You learn what the football team means to people."

It didn't take Holmgren long to understand that, especially after he encountered an elderly woman at a grocery the day before a game.

"She came up to me and said, 'OK, California, let's kick some butt,' " Holmgren said.

Ever since, Holmgren has tried to keep that simple phrase in mind. And every season since '92, the Packers had gotten a little bit better, gone a little farther, done a little bit more.

The biggest jump came in 1995, when the Packers won the NFC Central Division for the first time since 1972, shocked the defending Super Bowl champion San Francisco 49ers in the playoffs and reached the NFC title game, where they fell to the Dallas Cowboys.

But the 1996 season was different and

Mark Chmura and the Packers prepare to board their buses for the ride to the airport. For most road games, the Packers walk through the terminal to get to their flight. Instead, expecting a crush of well-wishers, they were driven directly to the plane. "This is a business trip." coach Mike Holmgren said. "I hope our fans understand that."

▲ Fans line the street as the Packers prepare to depart on buses for Austin Straubel International Airport and their journey to Super Bowl XXXI in New Orleans.

everyone could feel it.

"I drove this team hard and I drove my coaches hard because I felt we had something special here," Holmgren said. "I didn't want to leave any stone unturned."

It had fallen into place almost perfectly.

The Packers repeated as division champs, posted the conference's best record to seize home-field advantage and made the most of it by beating the 49ers and Carolina in the play-offs.

Now they stood on the threshold.

"There's still work to be done though," Reggie White said.

Following that plan, the Packers did nothing substantially different the week after clinching the NFC title. They knew they'd be facing the New England Patriots, led by the wily veteran coach Bill Parcells. The man had two Super Bowl titles under his belt as coach of the New York Giants.

And while Holmgren admitted he was probably the coaching underdog going into this game, he had some serious Super Bowl experience of his own, first as quarterback coach and then as offensive coordinator of the San Francisco 49ers.

As the national media converged on Green Bay, the Packers went about the task of putting in most of their game plan for the Patriots, realizing they wouldn't get a lot of quality work done in the circus atmosphere of New Orleans.

"We'll give them some new things just to keep their brains in gear," Holmgren said. "Then we'll start scaling back next week."

The idea was to have the bulk of the offensive and defensive plan in before the Packers left for Louisiana.

While that week in Green Bay was still business, Holmgren wanted to make sure his team knew something very important.

"I wanted them to enjoy the journey," he said. "They earned it. They should have fun."

Quarterback Brett Favre, who would be playing in the Super Bowl 60 miles from his home, planned to do just that. He dazzled the media that first week with a combination of wit and intelligence he'd rarely gotten a chance to show to anyone outside of Wisconsin.

When asked how far his hometown was from the Superdome, Favre said, "Exactly an hour driving. Going the speed limit, of course."

Favre joked about receiving ticket requests from people he hadn't talked to in years.

▲ Quarterback Brett Favre gets an up close and personal look from the cockpit of the Packers' charter flight.

▲ They left 20 degrees and snow and arrived to sun and 65. For the Packers, arrival in New Orleans meant it was finally time to get work.

▲ The crew of the Packers charter leaves little doubt who they're rooting for.

▲ The self-styled "three amigos": quarterback Brett Favre, tight end Mark Chmura and center Frank Winters.

"But now I've got friends I never knew I had," he said. "Now that I'm not a nobody."

Favre also was asked about his backup quarterback, Jim McMahon, who had been the starter 11 years earlier for the Chicago Bears when they beat the Patriots. In the Superdome. On January 26.

Favre said he and Mac discussed how ironic it was.

They also talked about McMahon's controversial behavior those days, when he mooned a helicopter that was trying to film a Bears practice and when he talked less than glowingly about the women of New Orleans.

"Actually, now I know exactly what not to do," Favre said.

For a team making its first Super Bowl appearance in 29 years, the Packers certainly seemed loose and confident. They also felt they were prepared for the media crush of Super Bowl week.

"We know it won't be anything like a normal week," wide receiver Antonio Freeman said. "We're going to go down there and enjoy ourselves, but we also know we're going down there for a reason."

"This is a business trip," Holmgren said.

But when defensive end Sean Jones was asked if they'd just as soon play the game that week instead of going through all the fuss, he smiled.

"No," he said. "We worked too hard to get here, so we might as well enjoy it for a while."

Perhaps no one was more appreciative of making another trip to the Super Bowl than wide receiver Don Beebe, who went to four straight with Buffalo and never experienced victory.

"I know how much it hurts to lose a Super Bowl," Beebe said. "To get another chance means everything to me. If we win, I may keep my uniform on the whole trip back."

The Packers worked out well that first week, practicing indoors at the Don Hutson Center to avoid the sub-zero temperatures.

On Sunday they left for New Orleans, arriving mid-afternoon to sunshine and 60-degree weather. It was here. Super Bowl week. At last.

"It finally hit me when the plane landed and there were 2,000 people (actually about 400) at the airport waiting for us," safety LeRoy Butler

◄ Mark Chmura decides to take a new look at practice during Super Bowl week.

▼ For Mike Holmgren, there is nothing more relaxing than a motorcycle ride. So he arranged with the New Orleans police department to do some riding after practice the Wednesday before the game.

Titletown Again

▲ Gabe Wilkins, contents himself with reading the newspaper while teammate Gilbert Brown is interviewed.

▲ The one regret coach Mike Holmgren had this season was that Robert Brooks wouldn't get the chance to play in the Super Bowl. "He's a special person," Holmgren said.

said. "We're finally here."

To their credit, the Packers handled the initial crush awfully well.

"We're trying to make this business as usual," Holmgren said. "The only difference today was that we were on a bigger plane, we watched a pretty good movie, the food was OK."

Asked what movie it was (that's a Super Bowl question, you see...) Holmgren fumbled around.

"Ummm...uhhh...it starred that guy who was in 'Speed,' " Holmgren said.

Informed that the actor in question was Keanu Reeves, and the movie was "Chain Reaction" Holmgren brightened considerably.

"Yeah, that's it," he said. "Good movie."

That was just a taste of what the Packers would have to deal with as 3,000 media representatives from 150 countries converged on the Big Easy to find a story no one had done before. Most would fail.

The questions, all kinds of questions, came in a withering, dizzying flurry.

What's it like living up to Lombardi's legend? Why are the Packers so good at home? Why are the Packers so bad on artificial turf? What's Brett Favre like? What's the most dangerous thing about the Patriots?

The Packers handled the onslaught admirably, though even the most good-natured players were starting to get sick of the attention by the end of the week.

"It's the same questions," cornerback Doug Evans said, shaking his head in amazement. "The same questions. I'd get finished with the question and then someone would come up and ask the exact same one."

Clearly one of the best stories involved Favre, who's hometown of Kiln, Mississippi, became a media mecca that week.

Expecting the onslaught, the town of 1,262 located hard by the Gulf of Mexico put on its best face. In fact, a media shuttle bus was organized to take the legion of writers, TV people and camera folks down to see where it all began for the Packers gunslinger.

"It's gotten bad," said Irvin Favre, Brett's dad and his high school coach. "It started about 8 o'clock in the morning. Man, they just bang on the door. I'm to the point where I

▲ The French Quarter makes its allegiances known.

▲ Halfback Edgar Bennett takes a break during practice at the New Orleans Saints training facility.

▲ Quarterbacks Brett Favre and rookie Kyle Wachholtz peruse a recent issue of Time magazine in which the Packers were the cover story.

▲ A sea of cameras, microphones, notepads and tape recorders greets Brett Favre at media day.

▲ Packer players look out at a sea of green and gold as they head to the Superdome for the game.

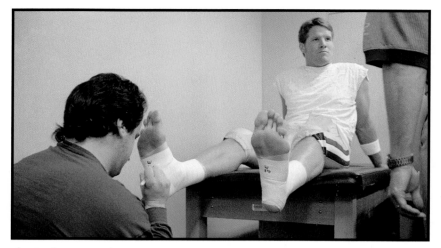

▲ Assistant trainer Kurt Fielding does his part to help the cause, writing a final score prediction on the bottom of Favre's taped feet.

▶ Running back Dorsey Levens relaxes before taking the field.

▲ Defensive end Gabe Wilkins takes a final look in the mirror before heading onto the field.

need to be Irvin Favre again, be a little more relaxed. So, hopefully, when I go up to New Orleans, it'll ease up some."

But for one week, Kiln became the biggest city in Mississippi as hundreds of fans and media poured into the community.

"We want to leave people with a favorable impresssion, not only of Brett and his family – but we try to promote the Green Bay Packers as much as we possibly can," Irvin Favre said. "I think we've done a pretty good job of that."

While Favre may have been the main focus of attention on the Packers side, New England coach Bill Parcells stole the spotlight on the other side.

In a Monday story in the Boston Globe, reporter Will McDonough said Parcells would quit the Patriots after the Super Bowl because of a deteriorating work relationship with team owner Robert Kraft.

At a turbulent Tuesday morning press conference, Parcells snapped and snarled at the Boston media, claiming that nothing in his relationship with the Patriots or Kraft had changed and that a decision would be made after the game.

The inquisition got fairly heated, and Parcells – not exactly a media charmer in the best of times – finally called a halt.

"That's the last question I'll take on that, gentlemen," he said.

And then: "Will this matter now be a distraction for your team?"

"Next question," Parcells grumped.

So it went.

Looking back, this may well have been a calculated ploy on Parcells' part, an attempt to take the pressure off his team (a staggering 14-point underdog according to Las Vegas oddsmakers), and place it on himself.

Whatever it was, Holmgren came out looking like Luke Skywalker to Parcells' Darth Vader.

At his press conference earlier that morning, the Packers coach had the media horde eating out of his hand with whimsical stories, self-deprecation and humor.

While Parcells was fielding razor-edged questions about his future, the toughest question Holmgren handled in his session was what he thought of the team's training facility in

▲ Brett Favre and Aaron Taylor joke around before the serious business of playing the Super Bowl.

▲ Coach Mike Holmgren makes a final point to his players as they get ready to play the New England Patriots. "I've shown you how to win this game," he told them. "Now go out there and do it."

▲ Andre Rison (right) and Antonio Freeman celebrate Rison's stunning 54-yard touchdown reception on Green Bay's second play from scrimmage.

▲ Edgar Bennett eludes the tackle of Mike Jones during one his runs. Bennett ran for 40 yards on 17 carries.

New Orleans.

He also regaled the media with stories of his early days as a high school history teacher and the unsuccessful football program at Sacred Heart High in San Francisco, where he lost his first 22 games.

"I was an assistant coach and working with my best friend," Holmgren said, explaining why he left that job. "I was newly married. We had little twins, so I had to get a job. The Christian Brothers, who run Sacred Heart, are wonderful. It's a wonderful order. But they believe in paying you with wine and not dollars."

The joint erupted in laughter.

In fact, Holmgren was in the process of amazing his players with the whole New Orleans show. The week before the Carolina game, Holmgren was wound tighter than most players had ever seen him.

"Coach can get heated sometimes," nose tackle Gilbert Brown said. "You can tell when it's coming around, so you better leave him alone."

Preparing for the Panthers, Holmgren made it clear he was going to be irritable and nervous.

"Some of the guys were kind of nervous and shaky," White said. "But Mike let us know

▲ Brett Favre is mobbed by teammates after running for a touchdown late in the first half that gave Green Bay a 27-14 lead.

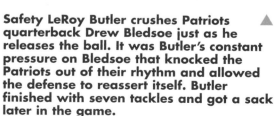

Safety LeRoy Butler crushes Patriots quarterback Drew Bledsoe just as he releases the ball. It was Butler's constant pressure on Bledsoe that knocked the Patriots out of their rhythm and allowed the defense to reassert itself. Butler finished with seven tackles and got a sack later in the game.

early in the week that he was going to be tense. He let us know he was going to approach it a certain way."

As a result, White called a players-only meeting to let everyone know that Holmgren, while an ogre for the moment, would calm down by game time.

"I mentioned to him that one of the things we talked about was that the guys feel you're too tense," White said. "Of course, his reaction was, 'Me? Who, me?'"

Holmgren smiled when reminded of the exchange, and replied, "I said to Reggie, 'Thank you...who are you calling tense?'"

In the week prior to the Super Bowl, though, the players noticed a distinct difference in their coach's demeanor.

"He's just a lot calmer," Freeman said.

Maybe it was because Holmgren knew that his Packers were ready. Not as ready as Holmgren could make them given the time, but ready, period.

Since July, Holmgren and his coaching staff had been molding and tinkering with this team and shaping it into a champion. Now the time had come and there was little more Holmgren could do.

Sometimes it seems like the Super Bowl, the

▲ The New England defense can only watch as Antonio Freeman heads down the sideline for a Super Bowl-record 81-yard touchdown that put Green Bay on top to stay. Chasing Freeman is rookie safety Lawyer Milloy while linebacker Chris Slade (53) observes.

◄ Brett Favre played as smart and controlled a game as he's ever played. He completed 14 of 27 passes for 246 yards, threw for two touchdowns, ran for one and didn't throw an interception.

game itself, will never arrive – that the hype will go on forever. And naturally that cycle repeated itself for the Packers and Pats.

But eventually, there's the game.

"It's time to play football," tight end Mark Chmura said on Thursday. "It seems like a month since we played a football game."

Everyone had done their analysis. The

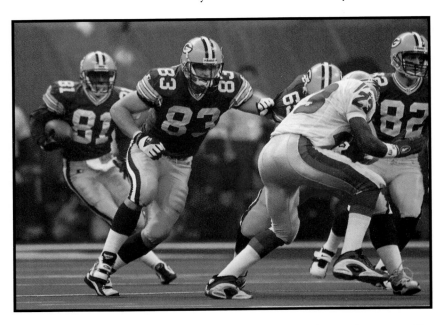

▲ The key play of the game. Desmond Howard watches as Jeff Thomason (83) helps open a hole. Howard squirted through the seam and ran 99 yards for the touchdown that shut down any momentum the Patriots had built.

▲ Brett Favre and Frank Winters celebrate Favre's two-point conversion pass to Mark Chmura that gave Green Bay a critical 14-point lead late in the third quarter.

experts weighed in with their opinions and anyone who cared even a little had made their best arguments as to why the Packers would win to continue NFC dominance, or why the Patriots would reverse the trend at last.

Holmgren had one final ace to play.

If fullback William Henderson's story is true, Holmgren placed what he said was $100,000 on a table during the team's Saturday night meeting. The idea was to demonstrate the approximate amount each player would make for the entire postseason if the Packers won the Super Bowl.

This was Holmgren's last appeal.

"For all those guys who aren't motivated by the rings, the glory, the championship and everything else, he had $100,000 set on the table," Henderson said. "I don't know what kind of bills they were, ones or tens. He said, 'For those of you moved by money, this is what you're looking at.' He covered everything else, too. It's a lot about pride. He mentioned that word."

Holmgren needn't have bothered. The Packers already knew what it was all about. They had something to prove and the time had come to put up or shut up.

The big day started superbly, too.

After holding the Patriots on their first series, Green Bay got great field position when Desmond Howard returned Tom Tupa's punt 32 yards to the Packer 45.

On first down, Edgar Bennett was stopped for a one-yard gain. The second-down call, part of Holmgren's 15 scripted plays to start the game, was supposed to be a five-yard square-out to tight end Keith Jackson.

But Favre saw a blitz coming and he liked the coverages he spotted on his wide receivers, especially Andre Rison. So Favre changed the play at the line of scrimmage, held up one finger to signal that Rison was the primary receiver, and went to work.

Matched up with cornerback Otis Smith, Rison turned Smith toward the sideline then broke sharply toward the post. Favre hit him with a perfect 54-yard strike for the touchdown.

Favre was exultant, pulling off his helmet and sprinting to the sideline with his hands in the air, then leaping into the arms of several players.

"It was man-for-man coverage and their man won on the route," Patriots defensive coordinator Al Groh said. "It was an audible check on their part against the man coverage look. We hoped to come out of that but, you know – kind of the jitters at the start of the game and the noise factor – we did not come out of it and they were able to take advantage."

Two plays later, from the New England 21, quarterback Drew Bledsoe tried to throw a sideline pattern to wide receiver Terry Glenn. But cornerback Doug Evans broke beautifully on the ball and made a juggling interception at the 28.

It looked like another NFC rout was in the making, but the Patriot defense rose up and stopped the Packers, forcing Chris Jacke to boot a 37-yard field goal, giving Green Bay a 10-0 lead less than six minutes into the game.

At that point, the Patriots changed tactics and knocked the vaunted Packers off-stride for a bit.

Instead of having Bledsoe take his normal nine-step drop and making him vulnerable to the Packers pass rush, Parcells had him take shorter drops and throw shorter passes that the receivers could turn into something bigger.

It worked splendidly.

On a second-down play, Bledsoe threw short to Keith Byars, who broke three tackles and rambled 32 yards to the Packers 47. Then Bledsoe tossed a screen pass to tailback Curtis Martin, who went 20 yards to the Green Bay 27.

After two incompletions, Bledsoe went for the end zone to Shawn Jefferson, where cornerback Craig Newsome was flagged for pass interference. On first and goal from the one, Bledsoe wasted no time, throwing a quick-hitter to Byars for the touchdown.

Suddenly confident, New England forced a three-and-out and surged right back on its next possession.

On third and one from the Packer 48, Bledsoe used a great play fake, Glenn slipped past safety Eugene Robinson and Bledsoe hit him for a 44-yard gain to the Green Bay 4.

A play later, Bledsoe found tight end Ben Coates, who got past linebacker Ron Cox, for a touchdown with 2:33 still remaining in the first quarter.

In less than eight minutes, a potential Packers rout was in danger of turning into a New England runaway. The 24 points set a Super Bowl record for most in a first quarter and Bledsoe's 15 pass attempts also set a record.

"They had us back on our heels," safety LeRoy Butler said. "No one had done that to us all season."

Defensive coordinator Fritz Shurmur wanted to make sure it wouldn't continue. After that second Patriot score, Shurmur gathered his

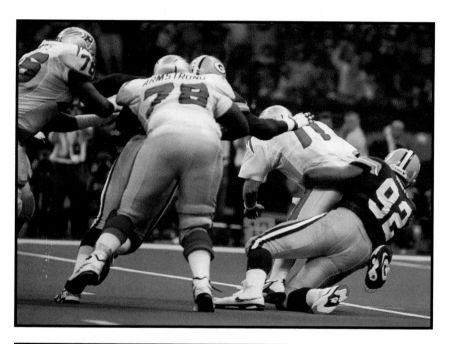

▲ Take one. Reggie White hauls down Drew Bledsoe with a key third-quarter sack.

◀ Take two. White gets to Bledsoe again on the very next play. White added a third sack later in the fourth quarter giving him three for the game, a Super Bowl record. (Photo by Chris Dennis)

defense together and told them to play like they meant it. He also told Butler to go after Bledsoe and let him know he was going to be around.

The strategy worked.

New England would have only 20 offensive plays from scrimmage the rest of the half and gain a mere 71 yards.

Meanwhile, Butler was coming on blitzes from his safety spot, while Evans and Newsome were making runs from cornerback, implanting the notion with the 24-year-old Bledsoe that he would be under siege.

While the defense seemed settled again, the Green Bay offense was badly off kilter.

After striking for 10 quick points, the Packers had bogged down and gained only six more yards in the first quarter. Favre was sacked twice.

Finally, on their second possession of the second quarter, the Packers caught the Patriots in a bad personnel matchup.

On first down from the Green Bay 19, Antonio Freeman found himself lined up on Pats rookie strong safety Lawyer Milloy.

"It's a tough-luck matchup for Lawyer," Groh conceded.

A touchdown's worth of bad luck.

Freeman easily beat Milloy's bump attempt at the line and Favre hit Freeman in stride at his own 45. It was a foot race from there, a race that Freeman was not about to lose.

The stunning pitch and catch covered a Super Bowl-record 81 yards, deflated the Patriots and ignited the Packers. Green Bay never trailed again.

The Packers kept the pressure on, thanks to Desmond Howard's 34-yard punt return that gave them possession on the New England 47. A 23-yard completion to Rison was the big play in the drive that finished with Chris Jacke booting a 31-yard field goal, making it 20-14 with 8:15 remaining in the first half.

Three plays later, Bledsoe tried to throw deep to Jefferson, but his pass was badly off-target and was picked off by safety Mike Prior.

Set up at the their own 26, the Packers zoomed downfield to the Patriots 2-yard line, thanks in part to a 22-yard completion from Favre to Freeman and 31 yards rushing in four carries by Dorsey Levens.

On first and goal, Favre swept left and headed for the pylon at the corner of the end zone. Though linebacker Todd Collins was closing in on him, Favre still managed to sneak the ball over the goal line for the touchdown and a 27-14 lead.

▲ Commissioner Paul Tagliabue (far left) presents the Vince Lombardi Trophy to team president Bob Harlan, general manager Ron Wolf and coach Mike Holmgren.

▶ Reggie White walks off the field holding the trophy he's sought his entire career. "Four years ago, a lot of people thought I was crazy for coming here," he said. "How crazy am I now?" (Photo by Russ Reaver)

▲ In the post-game media crush, Brett Favre still manages to find his seven-year-old daughter Brittany. (Photo by Chris Dennis)

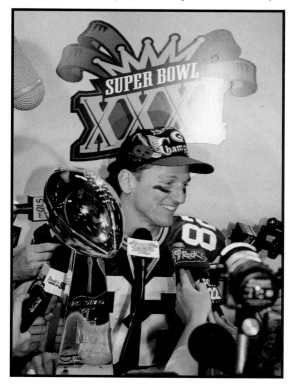

▲ Perhaps no one appreciated this Super Bowl title more than veteran wide receiver Don Beebe, who had been a member of four previous Super Bowl teams in Buffalo and lost them all. "Unless you've gone through it, you have no idea how much it hurts to lose," he said. "I may not need a plane to fly home."

▲ LeRoy Butler exults in the locker room afterward. Butler, in his seventh season, has the second-longest tenure of any Packer next to Chris Jacke.

◀ Finally, Andre Rison can smile. For years, he was tagged as uncoachable. But in Green Bay, he fit in perfectly. "This is the first time I've ever been on a team," he said.

Titletown Again

▲ Several members of the Packers take turns posing with an important piece of hardware on the trip home: Offensive coordinator Sherm Lewis, Reggie White, Super Bowl MVP Desmond Howard and defensive coordinator Fritz Shurmur.

The Patriots, who supposedly had to run on the Packers, had called just seven running plays by halftime and 1,000-yard rusher Curtis Martin had only 14 yards.

Bledsoe, meanwhile, threw 29 passes, completed 14 and had already been intercepted twice.

On the other side, the Packers felt the pendulum was swinging their way. The defense had pulled itself together and Favre, who had battled serious flu symptoms three days earlier, was playing in control. The rushing game had churned out 51 yards, just enough to keep New England honest.

On top of that, the Packers got the ball to start the third quarter and in their previous four games, the Packers had opened the second half with scores.

It seemed that would happen again as Green Bay started on its own 25 and moved smartly to the Patriots 37. But on fourth and a yard, Levens was dropped for a seven-yard loss, signaling a potentially critical change in momentum.

New England couldn't take advantage of the gift, at least not immediately.

But on their next possesssion, the Patriots made things exciting once again, driving from their own 47 to the Green Bay 18, where Martin blasted through a hole over right guard and ran in for the touchdown.

"We felt good about ourselves at that point," Patriots safety Willie Clay said. "We knew we were still in the game."

Not for long.

To Desmond Howard's amazement, the Patriots had kicked to him all day. He'd already hurt them with two scintillating punt returns that set up 10 Packer points.

And the Patriots did it again, kicking to Howard after Martin's touchdown.

"As I said over the course of the two weeks before this game, they can roll the dice and kick it to me if they want," Howard said. "But I have full confidence in my return team that they were going to allow me to pop one, because they've done it all year long. I didn't see any reason why our returns would be any different today."

Howard gathered in this kickoff at the 1-yard line, bolted straight up the middle, slipped two tackles and raced almost untouched for the touchdown that broke New England's back.

Don Beebe, Howard's deep mate on kickoff returns, could see early that the return had a chance to be something special.

"It was a middle return and we felt at the time we could get a kick," said Beebe, who returned a kickoff 90 yards for a touchdown against Chicago in October. "Either they kick it to me or to Desmond, and we felt that either one of us, we were going to score. We really did."

"When I came up, I was leading him and I saw how big the hole was. I said, 'Wow, we're going to score.' All I had to do was get on the safety, put my helmet in his pads, and then it's (Howard) and the kicker and there's no way the kicker's going to tackle Desmond in the open field. It's impossible. As soon as I made that block, I said he was going to score. I looked up, and there he goes."

Though Howard was surprised the Patriots kicked so consistently to him all day, Parcells didn't think he had many other options.

"We were worried about him, but you can't cancel the game," Parcells said. "I credit him. He really made the plays. Up until that point, I thought we still had an opportunity. But that hurt us and we couldn't close the deficit."

Instead of kicking the extra point, Favre convinced Holmgren to go for the two-point conversion, and he proceeded to hit Mark Chmura in the back of the end zone to give Green Bay a 35-21 lead.

Overall, Howard returned four kickoffs for 154 yards and six punts for 90 more. The combined 244 return yards set a Super Bowl record and earned Howard the game's MVP award – the first time in Super Bowl history a special teams player had earned that honor.

A pretty good case could have been made

for Reggie White, as well.

With a 14-point lead, White and the rest of the defense knew the Patriots had to throw to get back in the game. Plagued early by cut and chip blocks by the Patriots offensive line, White hadn't been able to do much. But as the game wore on and he sensed his first-ever championship, White's intensity surged.

Late in the third quarter, White began to open up the whole arsenal.

▲ It was just like Christmas as thousands of Packers fans lined the street in freezing temperatures to welcome home the Super Bowl champs.

▲ Don Beebe signals what the rest of the NFL already knows.

▲ Frank Winters and Mark Chmura acknowledge the crowd.

▶ Packers fans left a special gift for the city of New Orleans. Look closely and you'll see a new style of headware for the memorial erected to Louisiana soldiers who fought in the Spanish-American War. (Photo by Chris Dennis)

▲ Packer fans of all ages waited as buses carrying the players wound their way through town and to a celebration at Lambeau Field, where another 60,000 people waited.

On a second-down play, Reggie basically bulled over Pats right tackle Max Lane and sacked Bledsoe for an eight-yard loss. A play later, he ran around Lane and got Bledsoe again for a six-yard loss.

Then with 1:49 left in the game, White roared in again and picked up his third sack, setting a Super Bowl record.

"Now I can sit back with my son for years and watch the highlights of this Super Bowl, and he can see his daddy getting three sacks," White said.

And on the MVP matter, you could also argue the case for Favre.

He completed 14 of 27 passes for 246 yards, threw for two touchdowns and ran for another. Most important, he did not throw an interception.

"I don't know what else I've got to do to prove I'm a great quarterback," Favre said. "I'll go try to win the Pro Bowl, I don't know. I've done everything I can possibly do and I'm excited about that."

When Super Bowl XXXI ended and confetti rained down on the field, Holmgren was hoisted on his players' shoulders and led off the field in triumph.

The job was complete.

Afterward, the Packers reflected on what it meant to have attained a goal they had worked so hard and so long to achieve.

"Four years ago, a lot of people said I was crazy for coming here," said a beaming White. "How crazy am I now?"

"People have been counting us out all season," Freeman said, "and that's fine. But we're the world champions now and no one's going to take that away from us."

For Beebe, this was extra special. As he spoke to the media, clutching the Lombardi Trophy while still in full uniform, he could barely contain his emotions.

"This is great stuff, man," Beebe said. "I wish every football player could experience a Super Bowl championship and playing in Green Bay. You can't get any better than win-

ning a Super Bowl in Green Bay."

As for his promise to wear his uniform back to Green Bay if they won, Beebe smiled.

"I would," he said, "but I probably smell, so the guys won't let me."

Perhaps it was soft-spoken fullback William Henderson who best expressed the Packers' sentiments.

"We get to take a lot of pride back to Green Bay," Henderson said. "That's the main thing. The trophy is named after Mr. Lombardi. It's nice to take it back to his home. It's like we reinstated the legacy. It's the sweetest feeling in the world. It's like bringing a family heirloom back that's been gone for so many years."

▲ For a few days at least, thousands of Green Bay Packers fans turned the "The Big Easy" into "The Big Cheesy." (Photos by Chris Dennis)

Chapter 7
Somewhere, Vince Is Smiling

HAT WOULD VINCE LOMBARDI SAY ABOUT THE 1996 GREEN Bay Packers?

Would he cringe at the West Coast offense that places so much emphasis on throwing the football?

What would he think about Brett Favre? Could he deal with salary caps and free agency and the changing attitude of players these days?

What would he think of the tattoos that cover Andre Rison's body?

Could Lombardi coach this Packers team?

The answer, of course, is yes. This was the type of team Lombardi would have loved.

It had just the right mix of older veterans like Reggie White, Sean Jones, Mike Prior and Eugene Robinson, as well as players in the prime of their career — Brett Favre, Mark Chmura and LeRoy Butler. And their young, burgeoning stars such as cornerbacks Doug Evans and Craig Newsome, nose tackle Gilbert Brown and wide receiver Antonio Freeman.

But maybe that's not even the question that needs an answer any longer.

Finally, completely, totally, the Green Bay Packers, by virtue of winning Super Bowl XXXI, have emerged from those long shadows of history.

Still, coach Mike Holmgren thinks Lombardi would have appreciated this team, what it's accomplished and how it got there.

"It's a different time," Holmgren said. "We're working under a different set of rules in some instances. We have more players to deal with. But I know we believe in

some of the same things. I know we do. Commitment. Discipline. Great work ethic. Those are things I try to instill in my team. High-character people working very hard for a common goal."

The Super Bowl title was Green Bay's 12th championship, most in league history, but the first since it defeated the Oakland Raiders 33-14 in Super Bowl II in 1968.

Not even a month after that triumph, Lombardi stepped down as Green Bay's head coach, and Phil Bengtson took over. Soon after that, Lombardi left the Packers organization altogether to take over the floundering Washington Redskins. In his first season, the Redskins finished above .500 for the first time in 10 years.

A year after that, Lombardi was dead, the victim of cancer.

It is impossible to overstate the importance of Lombardi and the power he wielded. In many ways, the shadow Lombardi cast was this franchise's problem, making it impossible for anyone to live up the lofty standards he'd set.

Until that day in 1992 when team president Bob Harlan decided enough was enough.

Harlan decided to go after the best man available, give him the powers Lombardi had and allow him to rebuild this franchise.

That man was Ron Wolf, who wasted little time pursuing and signing Mike Holmgren as his head coach.

▲ The Packers' victory celebration flows into Milwaukee's Water Street. (Photo by Allen Fredrickson)

Since those two came on board, the Packers have not had a losing season, have gone to the playoffs four times, own a Super Bowl title and Green Bay is generally considered the class franchise in the NFL.

"I remember coaches threatening players by saying, 'If you guys don't shape up, we'll send you to Green Bay,'" Reggie White said. "It's not such a bad thing to do anymore, is it?"

The fans of the Green Bay Packers certainly didn't think so.

Think about them for a second.

It is now well-documented how special, how crazy, how completely devoted they are to their football team. But it goes beyond just supporting the Packers on Sunday afternoons.

These are fans that have been with the team through thick and thin, good times and bad. And they have always been there.

And is there a team that appreciates its fans more than the Packers?

Doubtful.

"They are the best fans in football," Brett Favre said.

The faithful proved that again the day after the Super Bowl. For a celebration billed as "Return to Titletown," 60,000 tickets were sold at $5 so fans could sit in Lambeau Field to honor their heroes. More than a million calls

were received from people trying to order tickets. And remember, this was before the game was played.

The plan seemed simple enough. The team would arrive back from New Orleans, they'd hop on buses, travel a parade route and end up at the stadium to receive their accolades.

It wasn't quite that easy. With Packer fans, it rarely is.

The parade route was choked with an estimated 200,000 people, and a motorcade that should have taken an hour from the airport to Lambeau Field took nearly three hours. Also, windows were removed from the buses so players and fans could interact. The wind chill was below zero, and by the time the team reached its destination, most players were nearly frozen.

But what the heck, right?

"You came out here in the freezing cold for this?" Beebe asked of the fans in general. "You're the greatest."

"We couldn't have done this without you," Holmgren said to the gathering. "Thank you for everything this season."

Howard may have drawn the biggest cheer.

"Yesterday after the game, they were talking about flying me to Walt Disney (World) today," he said. "But I told them it's not worth it if I can't share this whole experience with our

▲ **Don Beebe thanks the Packers Fans for their support during the "Return to Titletown" Celebration. (Photo by Allen Fredrickson)**

▶ **An emotional Desmond Howard acknowledges Packers faithful during the "Return to Titletown" Celebration. (Photo by Allen Fredrickson)**

fans. That's what the whole thing is all about, to bring it home to Green Bay."

So it's home.

"Coach Lombardi, I know you're listening," tight end Mark Chmura said. "Your trophy is safe once again."

But these Packers owe nothing to the past. They have been dogged by history and tradition from the moment they set foot in town and they knew what was coming.

They accomplished one of the toughest things in sports, which is winning when you're expected to win. As the Packers proved, that is

truly an impressive accomplishment.

Now what?

There is already talk of repeating and proving to anyone who still doubts that this season was no fluke. But changes are inevitable and some of the players who made 1996 so memorable have likely played their last game in a Packers uniform.

It is the nature of the beast and the Packers know this. You adjust, you do the best you can and you move on.

Holmgren told his players something like that in their final meeting together before they broke for all points on the compass.

"I wanted them to remember that one of the more difficult things to do in this league is repeat and come back with the same fire," Holmgren said. "But I expect they will."

It has been one of those seasons that won't be forgotten soon, a season in which a diverse group of individuals pulled together for one common goal. A season that saw a gunslinger from Mississippi and a preacher from Tennessee embrace in tears on the sidelines after the NFC title game. A season that saw a receiver go down at midseason with a knee injury yet stay around to offer encouragement and hope to the rest of the team.

It was a season that saw one linebacker, Ron Cox, lose his job to another (George Koonce) in training camp. But when Koonce was lost to injury in the playoffs, Cox stepped in seamlessly, telling Koonce, "I'm just doing your job until you get back." A season that saw a well-traveled wide receiver get a new chance in Green Bay and proclaim, "I've never felt so wanted in my life."

And it was a season that saw a franchise succeed by doing it the right way.

Perhaps San Francisco 49ers president Carmen Policy, whose club lost to Green Bay twice in the magic season, explained it best.

"We sense a very special relationship between the Green Bay community and their team," Policy said. "It's kind of a throwback to when things were simpler and purer, and I think what happened this year and the way it occurred is very, very good for the National Football League and professional sports in general. They did it the old-fashioned way."

And somewhere, Vince is smiling.

Season Statistics

Final Regular Season Statistics

	GB	Opp
TOTAL FIRST DOWNS	338	248
Rushing	118	74
Passing	197	151
Penalty	23	23
3rd down: Made/Att	97/219	74/226
3rd down %	44.3	32.7
4th down: Made/Att	5/11	14/22
4th down %	45.5	63.6
POSSESSION AVG	31:44	28:16
TOTAL NET YARDS	5535	4156
Avg per game	345.9	259.8
Total plays	1053	981
Avg per play	5.3	4.2
NET YARDS RUSHING	1838	1416
Avg per game	114.9	88.5
Total rushes	465	400
NET YARDS PASSING	3697	2740
Avg per game	231.1	171.3
Sacked/yards lost	40/241	37/202
Gross yards	3938	2942
Att/Completions	548/328	544/283
Completion %	59.9	52.0
Had intercepted	13	26
PUNTS/AVG	68/42.4	90/43.1
NET PUNTING AVG	68/36.3	90/32.5
PENALTIES/YARDS	92/714	107/797
FUMBLES/BALL LOST	33/11	25/13
TOUCHDOWNS	56	19
Rushing	9	7
Passing	39	12
Returns	8	0

Score by periods
PACKERS	76	125	136	116	3 —	456
OPPONENTS	32	96	25	57	0 —	210

Scoring
Jacke 114, Jackson 60, Levens 60, Freeman 54, Beebe 36, R. Brooks 24, Bennett 22, Howard 18, Favre 12, Mayes 12, Mickens 12, Rison 6, Butler 6, Evans 6, Henderson 6, Koonce 6.

Passing
	Att	Comp	Yds	Comp%	TD	Int	Long	sack/lost	rating
Favre	543	325	3899	59.9	39	13	80	40/241	95.8
McMahon	4	3	39	75	0	0	24	0/0	105.2

Rushing
	No.	Yds	Avg.	Long	TD
Bennett	222	899	4.0	23	2
Levens	121	566	4.7	24	5
Favre	49	136	2.8	23	2
Henderson	39	130	3.3	14	0
Jervey	26	106	4.1	12	0
R. Brooks	4	2	0.5	6	0
McMahon	4	-1	-.2	2	0

Receiving
	No.	Yds	Avg.	Long	TD
Freeman	56	933	16.7	51	9
Jackson	40	505	12.6	51	10
Beebe	39	699	17.9	80	4
Levens	31	226	7.3	49	5
Bennett	31	176	5.7	25	1
Chmura	28	370	13.2	29	0
Henderson	27	203	7.5	27	1
R. Brooks	23	344	15.0	38	4
Mickens	18	161	8.9	19	2
Rison	13	135	10.4	22	1
Howard	13	95	7.3	12	0
Mayes	6	46	7.7	12	2
Thomason	3	45	15.0	24	0

Interceptions
E. Robinson 6, Butler 5, Evans 5, Koonce 3, Newsome 2, White 1, Prior 1, Dowden 1, Hollinquest 1, Simmons 1.

Punting
	No.	Yds	Avg	Net	TB	Inside20	Long	Blocked
Hentrich	68	2886	42.4	36.3	9	28	65	0

Punt Returns
	Ret	FC	Yds	Avg.	Long	TD
Howard	58	16	875	15.1	92	3
Prior	0	1	0	0.0	0	0

Kickoff Returns
	No	Yds	Avg	Long	TD
Howard	22	460	20.9	40	0
Beebe	15	403	26.9	90	1
Levens	5	84	16.8	29	0
Henderson	2	38	19.0	23	0
Freeman	1	16	16.0	16	0
Jervey	1	17	17.0	17	0
Thomason	1	20	20.0	20	0

Field Goals
	1-19	20-29	30-39	40-49	50+
Jacke	0/0	6/6	9/11	5/9	1/1

Sacks
White 8.5, Butler 6.5, S. Dotson 5.5, S. Jones 5.0, Evans 3.0, Wilkins 3.0, Simmons 2.5, Gi. Brown 1.0, McKenzie 1.0, Clavelle 0.5, B. Williams 0.5.

Postseason Statistics

	GB	Opp
TOTAL FIRST DOWNS	53	40
Rushing	28	8
Passing	23	31
Penalty	2	1
3rd down: Made/Att	16/44	17/44
3rd Down %	36.4	38.6
4th down: Made/att	3/4	0/3
4th down %	75.0	0.0
POSSESSION AVG	35:25	24:35
TOTAL NET YARDS	1012	704
Avg per game	337.3	234.7
Total plays	198	179
Avg per play	5.1	3.9
NET YARDS RUSHING	455	156
Avg. Per game	151.7	52.0
Total rushes	120	45
NET YARDS PASSING	557	548
Avg per game	185.7	182.7
Sacked/yds lost	7/60	8/53
Gross yards	617	601
Att/completions	71/44	126/65
Completion %	62.0	51.6
Had intercepted	1	9
PUNTS/AVG	15/42.0	19/39.8
NET PUNTING AVG	15/35.5	19/27.7
PENALTIES/YARDS	9/91	12/89
FUMBLES/BALL LOST	7/2	5/3
TOUCHDOWNS	12	6
Rushing	4	2
Passing	5	4
Returns	3	0

Score by periods
PACKERS	24	41	25	10 —	100
OPPONENT	21	10	17	0 —	48

Scoring
Jacke 26, Bennett 18, Freeman 18, Howard 12, Rison 12, Favre 6, Levens 6, Chmura 2.

Passing
	Att	Comp	Yds	Comp. %	TD	Int	Long	sack/lost	Ratio
Favre	71	44	617	62.0	5	1	81	7/60	107.5

Rushing
	No.	Yds	Avg.	Long	TD
Bennett	59	219	3.7	13	3
Levens	39	195	5.0	35	0
Favre	14	35	2.5	12	1
Henderson	4	6	1.5	4	0
McMahon	4	0	0.0	0	0

Receiving
	No.	Yds	Avg.	Long	TD
Levens	10	156	15.6	66	1
Freeman	9	174	19.3	81	2
Rison	7	143	20.4	54	2
Jackson	5	44	8.8	19	0
Bennett	5	23	4.6	10	0
Chmura	3	28	9.3	15	0
Henderson	3	18	6.0	8	0
Beebe	2	31	15.5	29	0

Interceptions
Newsome 3, E. Robinson 2, B. Williams 1, Prior 1, T. Williams 1, Evans 1.

Punting
	No.	Yds	Avg	Net	TB	Ins	20	Long	Blocked
Hentrich	15	630	42.0	35.5	2	4		63	0

Punt Returns
	Ret	FC	Yds	Avg.	Long	TD
Howard	9	2	210	23.3	71	1
Hayes	1	0	0	0.0	0	0
Prior	0	1	0	0.0	0	0

Kickoff Returns
	No.	Yds	Avg.	Long	TD
Howard	9	277	30.8	99	1
Beebe	1	25	25.0	25	0

Field Goals
	1-19	20-29	30-39	40-49	50+
Jacke	0/0	1/1	4/4	0/2	0/0

Sacks
White 3, Butler 1, S. Dotson 1, Evans 1, McKenzie 1, Simmons 1.

Super Bowl XXXI – Play by Play

First Quarter

NE wins toss, elects to receive and GB elects to defend the north goal.
C. Hentrich kicks 67 yards from GB30 to NE3, H. Graham ret. to NE21 for 18 yards (K. McKenzie).

New England Patriots at 15:00
1-10-NE21   C. Martin right end to NE22 for 1 yard (B. Williams).
2-9-NE22   D. Bledsoe pass to S. Jefferson to NE36 for 14 yards (E. Robinson).
1-10-NE36   C. Martin right end to NE36 for no gain (B. Williams, R. Cox).
2-10-NE36   C. Martin up middle to NE36 for no gain (S. Dotson, G. Brown).
3-10-NE36   D. Bledsoe pass incomplete to D. Meggett.
4-10-NE36   T. Tupa punts 51 yards to GB13. D. Howard ret. to GB45 for 32 (L. Whigham).

Green Bay Packers at 12:19
1-10-GB45   E. Bennett left tackle to G46 for 1 yard (T. Johnson, W. McGinest).
2-9-GB46   **B. Favre pass to A. Rison for 54 yards and TOUCHDOWN.**
   C. Jacke extra point is GOOD. Center-J. Dellenbach. Holder-C. Hentrich.
NE 0, GB 7, 2 plays, 54 yards, 0:51 drive, 3:32 elapsed.
C. Hentrich kicks 72 yards from GB30 to NE-2, D. Meggett touchback.

New England Patriots at 11:28.
1-10-NE20   D. Bledsoe pass to C. Martin to NE21 for 1 yard. (G. Brown, C. Newsome).
2-9-NE21   D. Bledsoe pass intended for T. Glenn is INTERCEPTED by D. Evans at NE28 for no return.

Green Bay Packers at 10:40
1-10-NE28   B. Favre sacked at NE 38 for -10 yards (F. Collons).
2-20-NE38   D. Levens up middle to NE33 for 5 yards (F. Collons, M. Jones).
3-15-NE33   B. Favre pass to D. Levens to NE19 for 14 yards (T. Bruschi, J. Henderson).
4-1-NE19   **C. Jacke 37-yard field goal is GOOD. Center-J. Dellenbach. Holder-C. Hentrich.**
NE 0, GB 10, 4 plays, 9 yards, 1:58 drive, 6:18 elapsed.
C. Hentrich kicks 75 yards from GB30 to NE-5, D. Meggett ret. P-OOB at NE21 for 26 yards (T. Mickens).

New England Patriots at 8:42
1-10-NE21   D. Bledsoe pass incomplete to K. Byars (S. Dotson).
2-10-NE21   D. Bledsoe pass to K. Byars to GB47 for 32 yards (D. Evans).
1-10-GB47   D. Bledsoe pass to C. Martin to GB27 for 20 yards (B. Williams. C. Newsome).
1-10-GB27   D. Bledsoe pass incomplete to C. Martin. B Kratch called for illegal touch.
2-10-GB27   D. Bledsoe pass to T. Glenn (G. Wilkins).
3-10-GB27   D. Bledsoe pass incomplete to S. Jefferson.
GB-C. Newsome PENALIZED 26 yards for defensive pass interference. No play.
1-1-GB1   **D. Bledsoe pass to K. Byars for 1 yard and TOUCHDOWN.**
A. Vinatieri extra point is GOOD. Center-M. Bartrum. Holder-T. Tupa.
NE 7, GB 10, 6 plays, 79 yards, 1 penalty, 2:07 drive, 8:25 elapsed.
A. Vinatieri kicks 65 yards from NE30 to GB5, D. Howard ret. To GB18 for 13 yards (T. Ray).

Green Bay Packers at 6:35
1-10-GB18   E. Bennett right end to GB14 for -4 yards (C. Slade, L. Milloy).
2-14-GB14   D. Levens right tackle to GB17 for 3 yards (C. Slade).
3-11-GB17   B. Favre pass incomplete to A. Freeman (M. McGruder).
4-11-GB17   C. Hentrich punts 39 to NE 44, D. Meggett ret. To NE43 for -1 (B Harris).

New England Patriots at 4:44
1-10-NE43   D. Bledsoe pass to C. Martin to GB50 for 7 yards (W. Simmons).
2-3-GB50   C. Martin up middle to GB48 for 2 yards (G. Brown, R. Cox).
3-1-GB48   D. Bledsoe pass to T. Glenn to GB4 for 44 yards (E. Robinson).
1-4-GB4   **D. Bledsoe pass to B. Coates for 4 yards and TOUCHDOWN.**
A. Vinatieri extra point is GOOD. Center-M. Bartrum. Holder-T. Tupa.
NE 14, GB 10, 4 plays, 57 yards, 2:11 drive, 12:27 elapsed.
A. Vinatieri kicks 63 yards from NE30 to GB7, D. Howard ret. To GB26 for 19 yards (T. Bruschi).

Green Bay Packers at 2:33
1-10-GB26   B. Favre pass incomplete to A. Rison.
2-10-GB26   B. Favre pass to D. Levens to GB31 for 5 yards (T. Johnson, T. Collins).
3-5-GB31   B. Favre sacked at GB29 for -2 yards (T. Bruschi).
4-7-GB29   C. Hentrich punts 58 to NE13. Meggett ret. To NE33 for 20 yards (M. Prior).

New England Patriots at 1:03
1-10-NE33   D. Bledsoe pass incomplete to Glenn.
2-10-NE33   C. Martin up middle to NE38 for 5 yards (S. Jones).
3-5-NE38   D. Bledsoe pass incomplete to S. Jefferson (T. Williams).
4-5-NE38   T. Tupa punts 51 yards to GB11. D. Howard ret. to GB17 for 6 yards (M. Bartrum).

Green Bay Packers at 0:03
1-10-GB17   B. Favre pass to D. Levens, pushed out of bounds at GB21 for 4 yards (T. Collins).

Second Quarter

2-6-GB21   B. Favre pass incomplete to K. Jackson.
3-6-GB21   B. Favre pass incomplete to A. Rison.
4-6-GB21   C. Hentrich punts 37 yards to NE42. Downed by Packers.

New England Patriots at 14:39
1-10-NE42   D. Bledsoe pass incomplete to K. Byars.
2-10-NE42   D. Bledsoe pass incomplete to B. Coates.
3-10-NE42   D. Bledsoe pass incomplete to S. Jefferson.
4-10-NE42   T. Tupa punts 42 yards to GB16. D. Howard ret. To GB19 for 3 yards (D. Sabb).

Green Bay Packers at 14:14
1-10-GB19   **B. Favre pass to A. Freeman for 81 yards and TOUCHDOWN.**
   C. Jacke extra point is GOOD. Center-J. Dellenbach. Holder-C. Hentrich.
NE 14, GB 17, 1 play, 81 yards, 0:10 drive, 0:56 elapsed.
C. Hentrich kicks 68 yards from GB30 to NE2, D. Meggett ret. To NE24 for 22 yards (K. McKenzie).

New England Patriots at 14:04
1-10-NE24   D. Bledsoe pass to T. Glenn to NE33 for 9 yards (C. Newsome).
2-1-NE33   C. Martin up middle to NE36 for 3 yards (R. Cox, G. Brown).
1-10-NE36   D. Bledsoe pass incomplete to C. Martin.
2-10-NE36   C. Martin left tackle to NE39 for 3 yards (S. Jones, E. Robinson).
3-7-NE39   D. Bledsoe sacked at NE30 for -9 (L. Butler).
4-16-NE30   T. Tupa punts 51 yards to GB19. D. Howard ret. To NE47 for 34 yards (T. Ray).

Green Bay Packers at 11:13
1-10-NE47   E. Bennett right end to NE46 for 1 yard (D. Sabb, T. Law).
2-9-NE46   B. Favre pass to A. Rison, run out of bounds at NE23 for 23 yards.
1-10-NE23   D. Levens up middle to NE11 for 12 yards (L. Milloy).
1-10-NE11   E. Bennet right end to NE14 for -3 (L. Milloy).
2-13-NE14   B. Favre pass incomplete to D. Levens.
3-13-NE14   B. Favre pass incomplete to A. Rison.
4-13-NE14   **C. Jacke 31-yard field goal is GOOD. Center-J. Dellenbach. Holder-C. Hentrich.**
NE 14, GB 20, 8 plays, 33 yards, 2:58 drive, 6:45 elapsed.
C. Hentrich kicks 66 yards from GB30 to NE4, D. Meggett ret. to NE25 for 21 yards (B. Harris).

New England Patriots at 8:15
1-10-NE25   D. Bledsoe pass to B. Coates to NE44 for 19 yards (E. Robinson, R. Cox).
1-10-NE44   D. Bledsoe pass incomplete to K. Byars.
2-10-NE44   D. Bledsoe pass intended for S. Jefferson is INTERCEPTED by M. Prior at GB18. M. Prior to GB 26 for 8 return yards (T. Rucci).

Green Bay Packers at 7:10
1-10-GB26   B. Favre pass to K. Jackson to GB36 for 10 yards (C. Slade).
1-10-GB36   E. Bennett up middle to GB38 for 2 yards (T. Johnson, T. Collins).
2-8-GB38   B. Favre pass incomplete to A. Freeman.
NE-O. Smith PENALIZED 6 yards for defensive pass interference. No play.
1-10-GB44   B. Favre pass to A. Freeman to NE34 for 22 yards (L. Milloy).
1-10-NE34   D. Levens left end to NE25 for 9 yards (O. Smith).
2-1-NE25   D. Levens right tackle to NE19 for 6 yards (T. Collins, L. Milloy).
1-10-NE19   E. Bennett left end to NE18 for 1 yard (O. Smith).
2-9-NE18   D. Levens right end, pushed out of bounds at NE10 for 8 yards (T. Law).
Official time out at 2:00. Two-minute warning.
3-1-NE10   D. Levens right end to NE2 for 8 yards (W. Clay, T. Collins).
1-2-NE2   **B. Favre left end for 2 yards and TOUCHDOWN.**
   C. Jacke extra point is GOOD. Center-J. Dellenbach. Holder-C. Hentrich.
NE 14, GB 27, 9 plays, 74 yards, 1 penalty, 5:59 drive, 13:49 elapsed.
C. Hentrich kicks 72 yards from GB30 to NE-2, D. Meggett ret. to NE22 for 24 yards (L. Hollinquest).

New England Patriots at 1:06
1-10-NE22   D. Bledsoe pass to B. Coates to NE40 for 18 yards (L. Butler, M. Prior).
1-10-NE40   D. Bledsoe pass to T. Glenn to GB50 for 10 yards (E. Robinson).
1-10-GB50   D. Bledsoe pass to D. Meggett to GB49 for 1 yard (L. Butler).
2-9-GB49   D. Bledsoe pass to V. Brisby, pushed out of bounds at G42 for 7 yards (C. Newsome).
3-2-GB42   D. Bledsoe pass incomplete to T. Glenn.
4-2-GB42   D. Bledsoe pass incomplete to D. Meggett (E. Robinson).

Green Bay Packers at 0:19
1-10-GB43   B. Favre sacked at GB36 for -7 (W. McGinest).

Third Quarter

GB elects to receive and NE elects to defend the south goal.
A. Viniatieri kicks 68 yards from NE30 to GB2, D. Howard ret., P-OOB at GB25 for 23 yards (M. McGruder).

Green Bay Packers at 15:00
1-10-GB25   B. Favre pass to M. Chmura to GB33 for 8 yards (W. Clay).
2-2-GB33   E. Bennett right tackle to GB41 for 8 yards (L. Milloy).
1-10-GB41   B. Favre pass to W. Henderson to GB47 for 6 yards (T. Johnson).
2-4-GB47   W. Henderson up middle to GB49 for 2 yards (W. McGinest, P. Sagapolutele).
3-2-GB49   B. Favre pass to M. Chmura to NE46 for 5 yards (T. Law, T. ray).
1-10-NE46   D. Levens up middle to NE45 for 1 yard (C. Slade).
2-9-NE45   B. Favre pass to W. Henderson to NE37 for 8 yards (W. McGinest).
3-1-NE37   D. Levens up middle to NE37 for no gain (C. Slade, W. McGinest).
4-1-NE37   D. Levens right end to NE44 for -7 yards (T. Johnson, C. Slade).

New England Patriots at 9:32
1-10-NE44   D. Bledsoe pass to S. Jefferson to GB45 for 11 yards (D. Evans).
1-10-GB45   D. Bledsoe pass to K. Byars to GB41 for 4 yards (B. Williams, W. Simmons).
2-6-GB41   D. Bledsoe pass incomplete to B. Coates (S. Jones).
3-6-GB41   D. Bledsoe pass incomplete to S. Jefferson.
4-6-GB41   T. Tupa punts 29 yards to GB12, D. Howard fair catch.

Green Bay Packers at 8:07
1-10-GB12   B. Favre sacked at GB5 for -7 yards (O. Smith).
2-17-GB5   B. Favre pass incomplete to A. Freeman.
3-17-GB5   E. Bennett up middle to GB11 for 6 yards (M. Jones, L. Milloy).
4-11-GB11   C. Hentrich punts 48 yards to NE41, D. Meggett ret. To NE47 for 6 yards (T. Jervey).

New England Patriots at 6:52
1-10-NE47   C. Martin up middle to NE49 for 4 yards (G. Brown).
2-6-GB49   D. Bledsoe up middle to GB48 for 1 yard (S. Jones).
3-5-GB48   D. Bledsoe pass to B. Coates to GB35 for 13 yards (L. Butler, E. Robinson).
1-10-GB35   D. Bledsoe pass incomplete to C. Martin.
2-10-GB35   D. Bledsoe pass to S. Jefferson to GB26 for 9 yards (T. Williams).
3-1-GB26   C. Martin left tackle to GB18 for 8 yards (E. Robinson, D. Evans).
1-10-GB18   **C. Martin up middle for 18 yards and TOUCHDOWN.**
A. Viniatieri extra point is GOOD. Center-Mike Bartrum. Holder-T. Tupa.
NE 21, GB 27, 7 plays, 53 yards, 3:25 drive, 11:33 elapsed
A. Viniatieri kicks 69 yards from NE30 to GB1, D. Howard ret. 99 and TOUCH-DOWN.
Two-point conversion pass from B. Favre to M. Chmura is GOOD.
NE 21, GB 35, 0 plays, 99 yards, 0:17 drive, 11:50 elapsed.
C. Hentrich kicks 69 yards from GB30 to NE1, D. Meggett ret. to NE25 for 24 yards (J. Thomason).

New England Patriots at 3:10
1-10-NE25   D. Bledsoe pass to K. Byars to NE30 for 5 yards (W. Simmons, B. Williams).
2-5-NE30   D. Bledsoe sacked at NE22 for -8 (R. White).
3-13-NE22   D. Bledsoe sacked at NE16 for -6 (R. White).
4-19-NE16   T. Tupa punts 47 yards, out of bounds at GB37.

Green Bay Packers at 1:14
1-10-GB37   D. Levens right tackle to GB38 for 1 yard (C. Slade).
2-9-GB38   B. Favre right tackle to NE50 for 12 yards (W. McGinest).

Fourth Quarter
1-10-NE50   B. Favre pass incomplete to D. Levens.
2-10-NE50   D. Levens right tackle to NE49 for 1 yard (T. Johnson).
3-9-NE49   B. Favre pass incomplete to T. Mickens.
4-9-NE49   C. Hentrich punts 29 yards to NE20, fair catch D. Meggett.

New England Patriots at 14:03
1-10-NE20   C. Martin up middle to NE18 for -2 yards (E. Robinson, S. Dotson).
2-12-NE18   D. Bledsoe pass to T. Glenn to NE17 for -1 yard (G. Wilkins, D. Evans).
3-13-NE17   D. Bledsoe pass incomplete to S. Jefferson.
4-13-NE17   T. Tupa punts 53 yards to GB30, D. Howard P-OOB at GB40 for 10 yards (L. Whigham).

Green Bay Packers at 12:31
1-10-GB40   B. Favre pass to E. Bennett to GB44 for 4 yards (C. Slade, M. Wheeler).
2-6-GB44   E. Bennett up middle to NE46 for 10 yards (C. Slade, L. Milloy)
1-10-NE46   E. Bennett right end to NE48 for -2 yards (C. Slade, F. Collons).
2-12-NE48   B. Favre pass incomplete to A. Freeman.
3-12-NE48   B. Favre pass incomplete to M. Chmura.
4-12-NE48   C. Hentrich punts 34 yards to NE14, fair catch D. Meggett.

New England Patriots at 9:57
1-10-NE14   D. Bledsoe pass to B. Coates to NE17 for 3 yards (L. Butler, C. Newsome).
2-7-NE17   D. Bledsoe pass to D. Meggett to NE22 for 5 yards (W. Simmons).
3-2-NE22   D. Bledsoe pass to B. Coates to NE32 for 10 yards (L. Butler, E. Robinson).
1-10-NE32   D. Meggett right guard to NE32 for no gain (S. Dotson).
2-10-NE32   D. Bledsoe pass intended for S. Jefferson is INTERCEPTED by C. Newsome at GB31.
No return.

Green Bay Packers at 8:14
1-10-GB31   E. Bennett right end to GB31 for no gain (T. Collins).
2-10-GB31   E. Bennett right end to GB38 for 7 yards (C. Slade).
3-3-GB38   B. Favre pass to A. Freeman to GB40 for 2 yards (W. Clay).
NE-W. Clay PENALIZED 16 yards for unnecessary roughness.
1-10-NE44   D. Levens left end to NE37 for 7 yards (J. Henderson).
2-3-NE37   E. Bennett right tackle to NE36 for 1 yard (F. Collons, T. Johnson).
3-2-NE36   GB-B. Wilkerson PENALIZED 5 yards for false start.
3-7-NE41   D. Levens left tackle to NE34 for 7 yards (C. Brown, M. McGruder).
1-10-NE34   E. Bennett up middle to NE31 for 3 yards (T. Johnson, M. Wheeler).
2-7-NE31   E. Bennett right guard to NE30 for 1 yard (T. Johnson, M. Wheeler).
3-6-NE30   B. Favre pass incomplete to A Rison (O. Smith).
4-6-NE30   C. Jacke 47-yard field goal is no good, wide right.

New England Patriots at 3:36
1-10-NE37   D. Bledsoe pass incomplete to V. Brisby.
2-10-NE37   D. Bledsoe pass to D. Meggett, pushed out of bounds at NE39 for 2 yards (L. Butler).
3-8-NE39   D. Bledsoe sacked at NE32 for -7 yards (S. Dotson).
4-15-NE32   T. Tupa punts 37 yards to GB31, D. Howard ret. to GB36 for 5 yards (M. Bartrum).

Green Bay Packers at 3:11
1-10-GB26   E. Bennett up middle to GB30 for 4 yards (T. Johnson, W. Clay).
2-6-GB30   E. Bennett right tackle to GB34 for 4 yards (W. Clay).
3-2-GB34   B. Favre sacked at GB22 for -12 yards (T. Bruschi).
Official time out at 2:00. Two-minute warning.
4-14-GB22   C. Hentrich punts 54 yards to NE24, D. Meggett ret. to NE29 for 5 yards (T. Jervey).

New England Patriots at 1:49
1-10-NE29   D. Bledsoe sacked at NE20 for -9 yards (R. White).
2-19-NE20   D. Bledsoe pass incomplete to D. Meggett.
3-19-NE20   D. Bledsoe pass to V. Brisby to NE25 for 5 yards (C. Newsome).
4-14-NE25   D. Bledsoe pass intended for V. Brisby is INTERCEPTED by B. Williams at NE37, B. Williams to NE21 for 16 return yards (W. Roberts).

Green Bay Packers at 0:50
1-10-NE21   B. Favre up middle to NE22 for -1 yard.
2-11-NE22   B. Favre up middle to NE23 for -1 yard.
End of game.
Final Score GB35, NE21

The New America's Team
The Super Bowl Champion
Green Bay Packers

ROW 1 *(Left to right):* 2 Eric Matthews, 4 Brett Favre, 7 Kyle Wachholtz, 9 Jim McMahon, 13 Chris Jacke, 17 Craig Hentrich, 18 Doug Pederson, 19 Bill Schroeder, 21 Craig Newsome, 25 Dorsey Levens, 27 Calvin Jones, 28 Roderick Mullen, 30 William Henderson.

ROW 2: *Tight Ends/Assistant Offensive Line* Andy Reid, *Wide Receivers* Gil Haskell, *Offensive Line* Tom Lovat, *Running Backs* Harry Sydney, *Quarterbacks Coach* Marty Mornhinweg, *Offensive Coordinator* Sherman Lewis, *Head Coach* Mike Holmgren, *Defensive Coordinator* Fritz Shurmur, *Defensive Backs* Bob Valesente, *Linebackers* Jim Lind, *Defensive Assistant/Quality Control* Johnny Holland, *Defensive Line* Larry Brooks, *Strength and Conditioning* Kent Johnston, *Special Teams* Nolan Cromwell, 53 George Koonce.

ROW 3: 32 Travis Jervey, 33 Doug Evans, 34 Edgar Bennett, 36 LeRoy Butler, 37 Tyrone Williams, 39 Mike Prior, 40 Chris Hayes, 41 Eugene Robinson, 42 Buster Owens, 46 Michael Robinson, 51 Brian Williams, 52 Frank Winters, 54 Ron Cox, 55 Bernardo Harris, 56 Lamont Hollinquest, 57 John Solomon.

ROW 4: 59 Wayne Simmons, 62 Marco Rivera, 63 Adam Timmerman, 64 Bruce Wilkerson, 65 Lindsay Knapp, 68 Gary Brown, 71 Santana Dotson, 72 Earl Dotson, 73 Aaron Taylor, 74 Walter Scott, 77 John Michels, 80 Derrick Mayes, 81 Desmond Howard.

ROW 5: 82 Don Beebe, 83 Jeff Thomason, 84 Andre Rison, 85 Terry Mickens, 86 Antonio Freeman, 87 Robert Brooks, 88 Keith Jackson, 89 Mark Chmura, 90 Darius Holland, 91 Shannon Clavelle, 92 Reggie White, 93 Gilbert Brown, 94 Bob Kuberski, 95 Keith McKenzie, 96 Sean Jones, 98 Gabe Wilkins.

ROW 6: *Strength and Conditioning Assistant* Barry Rubin, *Corporate Security Officer* Jerry Parins, *Administrative Assistant/Football Offensive Assistant/Quality Control* Gary Reynolds, *Training Room Intern* Andre Daniels, *Assistant Trainer* Sam Ramsden, *Assistant Trainer* Kurt Fielding, *Head Trainer* Pepper Burruss, *Associate Team Physician* Dr. John Gray, *Team Physician* Dr. Patrick McKenzie, *Equipment Assistant* Tim Odea, *Equipment Assistant* John Odea, *Equipment Manager* Gordon 'Red' Batty, *Assistant Equipment Manager* Bryan Nehring, *Assistant Equipment Manager* Tom Bakken, *Equipment Assistant* Tim O'Neill, *Video Assistant* Chris Kirby, *Assistant Video Director* Bob Eckberg, *Video Director* Al Treml.